101

Easy, Effective and Exciting Evangelism Ideas

101 Easy, Effective and Exciting Evangelism Ideas

Copyright © 2014 by Nate and Erin Herbst

Scripture references quoted from NIV unless otherwise noted.

Printed in the United States of America

First Printing, 2014

ISBN: 978-1500150679

Master Plan Ministries
P.O. Box 1082
Durango, CO 81302

www.greatcommissionleadership.com
www.godsolutionshow.com
www.thebestfacts.com
www.christlikemen.com

facebook.com/neherbst

@eternityimpact

To George Wood.

Thank you for serving God and others with humility, gentleness, care and generosity. You and Dianne have been an incredible help to us and this ministry. You are a faithful man of God, a diligent prayer warrior and your heart for God and His Great Commission is contagious. Thank you for your example of lifestyle evangelism.

To Craig and Martine Stirling.

Thank you so much for your friendship and partnership in our lives and ministry. There is no way we would be where we are at in ministry if it wasn't for you. We love you!

Thank you Jesus for the privilege of sharing You with others!

Thank you Erin for your love and support.

Thank you Mom and Dad for demonstrating fearless and bold evangelism for me and helping me share my faith as a young boy.

Thank you Barbara Livingston, for the ministry and evangelism legacy you and Lyle have given our family.

Thank you Erin Herbst, Rhonda Denison, Angi Pratt and Austin and Laura Krokos for contributing to this book.

Thank you Russ and Linda Akins for keeping evangelism front and center in Master Plan Ministries.

Thank you MPM Staff for your commitment to Jesus and evangelism.

Thank you to all of our ministry supporters. Neither this book, nor this ministry, would be possible without you.

Thank you Meghan Renfro for the artwork!

Contents

"Success in witnessing is simply taking the initiative to share Christ in the power of the Holy Spirit and leaving the results to God. The only way we ever fail in our witness is if we fail to witness."[1]

Bill Bright

Forward

You do not need the gift of evangelism, in order to be good at sharing your faith. I am an introvert, and many people I have discipled over the years have also been introverts. I do not have the gift of evangelism, yet I have been able to share my faith and lead people to Christ. So have many of the people I have discipled during my time in ministry. You can do this too! Sharing your faith is scary; it is for almost everyone. Push through that fear and share your faith. Do not be afraid that you will not have all the answers. You have to start sharing your faith so you'll discover the questions people are asking and learn how to answer them. Learning to share your faith takes practice and preparation. That is the purpose of this book: to help you practice sharing your faith. You will make mistakes but the amazing thing is that even with the worst mistakes the Holy Spirit can still work. That is the point, you are not going out alone, the Holy Spirit is working with you.

Francis of Assisi once said "Preach always, use words if necessary." One of the many problems with this often used quote is that the poor fellow did not actually say it. It has been misattributed to him for all these years. The problem with using popular catch phrases, as life philosophies to follow, is that those catch phrases are not always in line with Scripture. For example, Romans 10:13-15 says, "For everyone who calls on the name of the Lord will be saved. But how can they call on Him they have not believed in? And how can they believe without hearing about Him? And how can they hear without a preacher? And how can they preach unless they are sent? As it is written: How beautiful are the feet of those who announce the Gospel of good things!" (HCSB). So, according to Scripture, if we do not use words people will not be able to call on the name of the Lord.

There is a massive revival happening all over the world. China will soon be the largest Christian nation in the world. Yet in the West, it appears that our nations are becoming "post-Christian." Why is this? Is it because people in other nations around the world are more hungry for the Gospel? I do not think so. I believe it is because only a handful of Christians are actually sharing the Gospel in the West. If we sow the Gospel sparingly, people will come to Christ sparingly (Matt. 13:1-23). Christians in places like China are sharing the Gospel, even at a great cost to themselves. Yet here in the United States, Christians are focusing the majority of their efforts on not offending people. We come up with fancy programs, trendy causes, and so-called "friendship evangelism" in order to win "seekers" to Christ. Unfortunately, it appears that non-Christians, in this country, are responding to this "technique" by becoming more offended and less willing to come to Christ. That is because we have left the simplicity of sharing the Gospel.

Nate and I once heard a speaker talking about the Parable of the Sower (Matt. 13:1-30). He asked what kind of a farmer would sow on rocks, a road and among thorns. He then answered his own question stating, "A stupid one." After the laughs subsided he exclaimed, "God doesn't call us to be soil specialists, He calls us to be seed chuckers." All God is asking you to do is to share His Good News often, boldly and broadly.

If you are reading this book, it is because you want to share the Gospel. You can do it! Take these ideas and apply them. My grandmother Barbra always prays, "Lord take me or use me," and guess what, God uses her! Her desire to be used and her willingness to trust God have led to many new believers. God will use you too if you are willing. You will make mistakes, some may even get offended, but you will find that even people in this country are hungry for Christ and once they hear the Gospel, many will come to Him. You are embarking on a life-changing adventure that I hope will continue for the rest of your life. You have nothing to lose and the people you will lead to Christ have everything to gain. I hope you get a ton out of this short book.

Erin Herbst, June 19, 2014

Introduction

Thank you so much for giving this book a chance! I know your life will never be the same. God is doing great things all around the world but right here in this country, His followers are suffering from the deadly affliction of evangophobia. Infinitesimally small numbers of believers are following His command to preach the Good News to those around them. Most believers are filled with unbelief about evangelism and our society is beginning to reap the results of our negligence and disobedience.

People all around us are dying in a spiritual desert while most Christians, instead of offering them spiritual water, are trying to make Christ's message as much like the desert as possible, so as to not offend anyone. The people you encounter each day, your neighbors, co-workers, friends and relatives, need pure spiritual water. It is critically important that you give them Christ, not some socially acceptable Christ-mannequin dressed up with all that's new and trendy in our culture. This has become our reality in much of the West, but thank God this is not the case everywhere.

God is moving around the world! It is hard to nail down exact statistics about all God is doing globally. These statistics, though imperfect, give us a glimpse of the progress of Christ's Great Commission. These statistics are also likely underestimates as no one knows the full extent of all that is happening throughout the world. The following statistics paint a vague but encouraging picture of the global revival occurring today. The Traveling Team, a powerful Great Commission focused ministry, states that over 260,000 people hear the Gospel and more than 174,000 trust Christ worldwide every single day, including 34,000 in South America, over 30,000 in China and 25,000 in Africa every day.[2] A Muslim source even begrudgingly admits that there are 16,000 Muslims coming to Christ each day in Muslim countries around the world![3] For a picture of some of that, visit greatcommission2020.com. That is exciting but there is still so much to do. That is where you come in.

God put you in your sphere of influence, at this very time and in this very place so that people would come to know Him (Acts 17:26-27). He does not want a single person to be lost (2 Peter 3:9) but wants everyone to be saved (1 Tim. 2:4); you are His tool for accomplishing that goal in your area. The harvest is really very ripe (Matt. 9:37) and people have no other answers. Paul writes, in 1 Corinthians 9:16, "if I preach the Gospel, I have nothing to boast of, for I am under compulsion; for woe is me if I do not preach the Gospel" (NASB). We were made to witness and just like a fish can't live out of water, a Christ follower can't help but share the Good News. If you will commit to a lifestyle of evangelism you are guaranteed to impact people and eternity for Christ.

Unfortunately, so many American Christians doubt and diminish the issue of hell, oblivious to all that is at stake. The result has been decreased motivation for evangelism. Sadly, many Christians seem to be following their own thinking more than Scripture on this topic. Hell is real, it will be terrible and it will be eternal. Real people that you know and love will spend eternity there if they don't come to Christ. The Bible describes hell as a real and eternal place that will be horrible. Don't over or underemphasize hell, and don't ignore it. Do everything that you can to "save others, snatching them out of the fire" (Jude 1:21-23 NASB). Also remember that it is God's kindness that draws people to repentance (Rom. 2:4). The reality of hell should motivate believers to share the Gospel while Christ's love and grace should be the focus of our evangelistic message.

Don't get discouraged if you don't see fruit right away. Remember that success in evangelism is simply being faithful. MPM staff lady Leah Hillewaert has been sharing her faith for years and recently got to lead her first person to Christ. Way to keep at it Leah. Follow her example and keep persevering regardless of results.

Keep going when you face opposition. My dad was actually arrested while sharing his faith, along with several ministry partners, in Las Vegas in 1973. They were all thrown in jail for witnessing in front of casinos. That turned into an incredible time of fellowship for them (they even had communion together in jail) and a rallying point for local believers. Our ministry has even faced administrative opposition to evangelism on the college campus as well. We recently had to get legal help to challenge a policy made to limit evangelism on campus. The campus tried to write a solicitation policy to stop most evangelism on campus. Thank God they backed down when our talented lawyer, Lori Kepner, challenged the policy. You should also expect to face opposition from Christians. Many of them will be threatened by your commitment to Christ and His Great Commission. Love them and keep sharing your faith. Don't back down from opposition. Expect it, fight through it lovingly and in the power of the Holy Spirit and keep going, trusting God and sharing the Good News.

The harvest is ripe but the workers are few (Matt. 9:37-38). I have designed this book with the hope of equipping you with a strategy and ideas for evangelism. This book is not exhaustive, but it is a good start. I hope it gives you some decent rails to run on as you strive to reach your sphere of influence for Christ. I know the ideas and strategies it contains will help you do that. You will undoubtedly experience unparalleled joy in evangelism as you follow Christ's example of evangelism, putting these ideas into practice.

Finally, this book will help you love Jesus better, by following His commands, and it will help you love your neighbors as yourself, by equipping you to meet your neighbors' greatest spiritual needs. As you seek to do that, remember that you don't have what it takes but the Holy Spirit in you does. He will empower you for bold evangelism as you simply step out in faith, trusting Him (Acts 1:8). Enjoy this book and share it with Christian friends who could use the encouragement. Thanks for reading it!

Chapter 1

Five Keys to SHARE Your Faith

"I'm just a nobody trying to tell everybody, about somebody, who can save anybody."⁴ - Lyrics From a Williams Brothers song

The goal of this book is to resource you with great ideas for sharing your faith. Paul told Timothy, "...preach the Word; be prepared in season and out of season..." (2 Tim. 4:2). The charge is the same for you today! People all around you are desperately searching. Several years ago, the boyfriend of a young lady I had led to Christ told me, "I will kill myself tonight if you don't tell me how I can get right with God." This was a very successful young man, plagued by guilt about all he had done to achieve his goals. A few hours later, he, his girlfriend, Erin and I prayed together with him as he put his trust in Christ. There are people just like that around you today. They might not come right out and say it but they are searching for Jesus. It is important that you have an evangelistic strategy in place so you don't miss opportunities like that one.

I want to begin this book by giving you a short evangelism strategy that you can use anywhere and anytime. You don't have to be anyone special, "just a nobody trying to tell everybody, about somebody, who can save anybody" is fine! This strategy will help you do that; it always works. I'll share the SHARE acronym with you in this chapter and I know it will change your life if you memorize and apply it.

Keith Davy describes three modes of evangelism[5] that, if understood, can help you better understand how to share your faith. The first mode is the "Body Mode." This is a simple way to reach people for Christ. It involves inviting them to Christian events (a church service, concert, etc.) and then letting them experience the Body of Christ. The second mode is the "Relational Mode." This involves sharing Christ in your existing friendships, throughout the natural course of those friendships. The last mode is the "Ministry Mode." This involves sharing Christ intentionally as a ministry activity, most often with people you've never yet met. This can be awkward but it is the type of evangelism that we see most often in Scripture and it is often times the best way to grow in your witnessing abilities. All three modes are effective and each should be present in a lifestyle of evangelism.

The **SHARE** acronym works with all three and it is especially helpful with the ministry mode that tends to scare most people. Again, memorize this acronym and make it a point to apply this in your daily life. As you work through the ideas in this book, do them in the context of this acronym. This strategy is a simple way of remembering an effective approach to personal evangelism. SHARE stands for Supercharge, Have an expectant attitude, Ask questions, Resources and Encourage them. Let's get into each of those issues a little more in depth.

Supercharge. Acts 1:8 tells us that the Holy Spirit empowers believers for bold evangelism. I love acronyms so I'm going to throw another one at you. The POWER acronym for being filled with the Spirit will remind you how to walk in His power each day and especially when you're witnessing. You can walk in the power of the Holy Spirit each day by:

Presenting yourself to God, surrendering to Him (Romans 12:1-2).

Owning up to any sin God makes you aware of, confessing it to Him (1 John 1:9).

Wanting to live a Christ-like, Spirit-filled and empowered life (Matthew 5:6).

Experiencing His filling and power, claiming it by faith alone through prayer (James 1:6-7, 1 John 5:14-15).

Relying on Him, taking steps of faith that require Him to come through (2 Cor. 5:7).

Before witnessing, consciously ask God to fill you with His Holy Spirit, empowering you to witness with His power and authority. Pray for those you will share with (remember the "Divine Order"). Then step out, supercharged with His power, trusting Him to work in other people's lives through you.

Have an expectant attitude. Look for opportunities and expect God to use you in great ways! Do not share your faith with a "no one will be interested, no one will respond, no one wants to hear this" attitude. One of Spurgeon's first students, Mr. Medhurst, once complained to him that after three months of evangelism he didn't know of a single person who had come to Christ. Spurgeon answered, "you don't expect conversions every time you open your mouth, do you?" Stunned, Mr. Medhurst capitulated, "Of course not!" Spurgeon then shocked him even more, stating, "Then that is just the reason you haven't had them."[6] An expectant attitude is imperative in evangelism.

Go out excited to see all God will do! Your attitude will effect your willingness to obey God, the frequency with which you obey Him, the way you come across to those you share with and every other aspect of evangelism. Don't let a lack of results, opposition to your efforts or any other circumstances quell your enthusiasm. One young man I shared with was so opposed to Christ I felt he would never trust Christ. A year later, I was able to lead him to Christ and am now discipling him. He is also planning to go into full time ministry. Remember stories like that one when you feel your evangelism was ineffective. Don't let anything sidetrack you from the reality that God will always produce fruit when you serve Him (1 Cor. 15:58). Determine today to share your faith with a joyful and expectant attitude taking the "initiative to share Christ in the power of the Holy Spirit and leaving the results to God." [7]

Ask questions. In chapter three, in the second evangelism idea, I'll share how to use transition questions to transition any conversation to the Gospel. For now, just remember that you can transition any conversation to the Gospel, in simple and non-awkward ways, and questions are the key to doing that! Think of a few conversation starting questions you could use to get into conversations with people. Then, think of good questions that can transition to a conversation about Christ. A great example is, "What's been your experience with Christianity?" Learn to carefully, authentically and genuinely listen to people's answers, as good listening will help you find conversational transition points and build bridges with those you want to share the Good News with. It is vitally important that you make creative questions and thoughtful listening key components of your evangelism strategy.

Resources. Use resources that will help you confidently share your faith and train the next generation of people you're discipling to as well. We call these transferable resources. A great example is the KGP (Knowing God Personally) booklet, available from crupress.com. Gospel presentations like this are conversational tools that help millions of people each year put their faith in Christ. Don't shun such powerful and transferable tools, just learn how to use them in relational and non-awkward ways. This book will equip you with a ton of ideas, which are also resources for evangelism; ideas are important and they must fit within the greater SHARE framework of personal evangelism.

The most important thing about resources is presenting a complete description of the Gospel and an opportunity to respond. Good resources do this. It is critical that you share God's love for the person you are witnessing to. Jesus included this in His Gospel message (Jn. 3:16). You can see Jesus' Gospel presentation in Evangelism Idea #93. You must also adequately explain the sin problem. Until someone understands that, they won't see the need for forgiveness. Especially in this day and age, where sin has been nearly completely written off, it is necessary that the person come to understand how their selfishness and imperfection have separated them from our perfectly loving God. They must also understand that sin separates us from God now, and left unmitigated, it will separate us from Him for eternity. Once the sin issue is understood, people must hear of God's only solution for that dilemma, Jesus and his payment for our sins on the cross. Finally, they must realize that they have a choice to make, to put their faith in Jesus, receiving His gift of salvation, or to reject Him and all that He offers. If they choose to put their faith and trust in Christ, they must verbalize that (Rom. 10:9) and can do that through prayer, praying a simple prayer like, "Jesus, I know you are who you say you are and that you died on the cross for my sins. I believe you rose again to give me new life. I ask you to come into my life as my Savior and Lord. Please make me the kind of person you want me to be." That's not a silly prayer or a magic button but a way of verbalizing their faith in Christ in a way that Scripture says is necessary for salvation. Every Gospel presentation must include these fundamentals and most good resources will.

As you use resources, be up front with those you talk to about what you're doing. For example, if you're using a survey, mention that it is a spiritual interest survey and that you are a part of a Christian group trying to survey people. Don't trick people into listening to a Gospel presentation. Nobody likes the bait and switch technique. Be honest about what you're up to and respect their choice to listen or not.

Encourage them! Be ready to implement a follow-up plan right away. Whether someone puts their trust in Christ or is interested in hearing more, plan to meet up with them again to encourage them towards Christ. Get their contact information before leaving and don't delay in setting up a follow-up appointment. It is a shame how many hungry seekers are never followed up with and it is just as tragic when new believers are not discipled. Don't make either of these mistakes!

So there you have it, the SHARE acronym. If you will supercharge before witnessing, going out in the power of the Holy Spirit rather than trusting your own abilities, you will see fruit in evangelism. If you have an expectant attitude, you'll have tremendous joy in witnessing and will see God use you in greater ways than you can imagine. If you learn to ask questions in evangelistic conversations, you'll find yourself transitioning all sorts of conversations to the Gospel. If you add resources to all that you'll be powerfully equipped to share your faith anytime and anywhere with anyone. Finally, if you encourage those you share with, following up with those who are interested and discipling those who put their trust in Christ, you will see a constant flow of new believers flowing from your ministry. Implement this SHARE acronym in your life and ministry and you won't believe all God will do in and through you.

There is a world in desperate need of a Savior and you are God's plan for reaching those around you. There is no plan B. Boldly share the Gospel as you should (Eph. 6:19-20) and set an evangelism example for your Christian friends as well.

"If you believe that there's a heaven and hell and people could be going to hell or not getting eternal life, or whatever, and you think, 'well, it's not worth telling them this because it would make it socially awkward' … How much do you have to hate somebody to not proselytize? How much do you have to hate somebody to believe that everlasting life is possible and not tell them that?" [8] *- Penn Jillette (a famous atheist)*

The Gospel is "the power of God for the salvation of everyone who believes" (Rom. 1:16). God does not want anyone to perish but instead wants everyone to come to repentance (2 Peter 3:9); He wants everyone to come to salvation (1 Tim. 2:4). Since you're reading this book, I am sure you're not the kind of person who is full of unbelief about evangelism (if you were, I doubt you would have made it this far). This chapter will equip you to recognize the lies that keep so many from sharing the Good News. Catch these in your own life and make others aware of them too.

Christ came to seek and to save the lost (Lk. 19:10) and He has put you and I here for that same reason (Acts 17:26-27). Scripture is clear, anyone who puts their trust in Christ will be saved (Jn. 3:16, Acts 2:21, Rom. 10:13). The harvest is plentiful but the workers are few (Matt. 9:37). We are the workers He has chosen to use and it is time for us to win this world for Him! Don't ever let Satan's lies stop you from that.

There are so many different lies that have kept Christians from sharing the Good News. There are ten that are particularly destructive (but these are by no means the only ones). I think it is important to get these lies out in the open right off the bat so they aren't messing with you the rest of this book. Here they are in no particular order.

Lie #1 - You must have the gift of evangelism. Many don't share because they don't feel like they have that gift. We would never say you must have the gift of hospitality in order to be hospitable, the gift of giving to give or the gift of encouragement to encourage. Some will have the gift of evangelism but we're all called to share the Good News. Remember Matthew 4:19; if you follow Christ you're called to evangelism! Don't ever believe the lie that you have to have the gift of evangelism in order to share.

Lie # 2 - Your personality, skill, knowledge, looks, style, and actions validate the Gospel and make it relevant. Many Christians don't witness because they feel they aren't good enough Christians. The whole point of the Good News is that we are sinners that need a Savior! 1 Corinthians 1:27 says that God chooses the foolish and weak things of this world to glorify Him. He doesn't need you to "validate" the Gospel (you should definitely do your best not to invalidate it through hypocrisy). Also, many people don't share because they don't think they have all the answers. You never will!

Do your best to prepare and then trust Him. Don't believe the lie that the power of the Gospel rests on your performance or abilities.

Lie #3 - You must earn the right to be heard. Another version of this goes, "they don't care how much you know till they know how much you care." That is definitely true for leadership and discipleship, but not for evangelism! Jesus earned the right to be heard two thousand years ago. He also earned the right to be obeyed by His followers; He claimed to have all the authority to command us to witness (Matt. 28:18-20, Acts 1:8). Many people incorrectly believe you must befriend people before witnessing to them. The number one reason people reject the Gospel is because of hypocritical Christians; the "friendship only" approach isn't working. Jesus called us to reach the whole world. This would be practically impossible if everyone had to be befriended first. Imagine how long it would take to befriend the entire world before sharing with them. Be friendly but also be open to sharing with anyone God puts in your path. There are very few, if any, places in Scripture, where anyone befriended someone before sharing with them. Love people and share with them. Don't believe the lie that you can't share the Gospel with someone until some level of friendship has been attained.

Lie #4 - Booklets and pamphlets should be avoided. Romans 1:16 tells us, "I am not ashamed of the Gospel, because it is the power of God for the salvation of everyone who believes..." The Gospel message is powerful, whatever its format. Gospel "tracts" and pamphlets can be great conversational tools and they can be transferable resources that make it easier for people you're discipling to learn how to share their faith. It is important to personalize these tracts as much as possible. You should never believe the lie that God can't use them.

Lie #5 - The poor, needy, and destitute are those we should focus evangelism on most. We must remember that the rich are lost too (Matt. 19:23-24)! The poor are, without question, close to God's heart and we should do everything we can to help them but they aren't the only ones God wants to reach. The poor and the rich alike are lost without Jesus and we should strive to share the Good News with them all! Don't believe the lie that rich people are fine the way they are and the destitute are the ones who really need spiritual help. Everyone needs Jesus!

Lie #6 - It is your responsibility to make sure no one gets offended. Jesus promised men would hate you because of Him (Matt. 10:22)! Scripture also tells us we will be disgusting to some, but life to others (2 Cor. 2:16)! Share in a loving and truthful way and then trust the results to God. Gregory Koukl writes, in *Tactics*, "Jesus' teaching made some people furious. Just make sure it's your ideas that offend and not you, that your beliefs cause the dispute and not your behavior."[9] Be loving and truthful and remember, if people get offended, that is not your problem. Trust God with your insecurities. Don't believe the lie that you can or should even try to make people like you all the time.

Lie #7 - Methods are what produce results. Jesus said that it was the amount of seed sown that led to larger harvests (Matt. 13:1-9). We should always be looking for great new evangelism tools but must remember sharing the Good News is the key to reaching people for Christ. Never put off sharing your faith while you wait for better tools or ideas. Sow lots of seed in lots of places lots of different ways. Don't believe the lie that you need to find some special evangelism "magic bullet."

Lie #8 - "Preach always, use words if necessary." This is a popular misquote of St. Francis of Assisi. There are good Mormons, Buddhists, witches, and atheists; good works don't save people or show people the way to eternal life. We should live such godly lives that people will see Christ in us (1 Peter 2:12) but we must also remember that words are necessary (Rom. 10:13-14). We should both share the Gospel and live lives that show people Christ, not one or the other. Don't believe the lie that good works alone are a sufficient evangelistic approach.

Lie #9 - Older people are stuck in their ways and won't trust Christ. On the contrary, dreams forgotten, relationships broken and the ends of their lives approaching, many have never been more desperate. Remember John 12:32-33; Jesus is drawing every person to Himself! That includes the old. Don't believe the lie that you shouldn't try to reach all ages of people for Christ.

Lie #10 - Most people aren't interested in spiritual issues and hearing the Gospel. Jesus tells us, in Matthew 9:37, "The harvest is plentiful but the workers are few..." Workers are the limiting factor in the harvest. It is time to quit believing lies and start working in the harvest God has put us here for! Don't believe the lie that people aren't interested in Jesus.

Remember, James 1:22 tells us that disobedience leads to deception. The reason many of these evangelism lies are so prevalent today is because most Christians are not obeying the command to share their faith. Their disobedience is leading to deception. Don't believe these ten lies or any others. Trust God will use you mightily if you'll just obey Him by sharing your faith!

I think most of these lies are really just excuses. Ultimately, fear is the main reason most people fail to share their faith. People can come up with a million excuses, justifications and rationalizations for not witnessing but no matter how legitimate and spiritual they sound, they all boil down to fear. Learn to fearlessly trust God, obeying Him and sharing the Good News!

Here are five keys to crushing fear so it won't keep you from evangelism. First, conquer fear by fearing God. A correct view of God will displace all other fear (He is bigger than anything you could possible fear). Fear God, respect Him for who He really is, instead of fearing whatever else is causing you fear (Mt. 10:28). Second, conquer fear by dying to yourself. Having been crucified with Christ (Gal. 2:20), you are free to live by faith rather than fear. Third, conquer fear by knowing and applying God's Word. Joshua 1:8-9 connects courage with a knowledge of God's Word. If you're letting fear stop you from evangelism, you're definitely getting your eyes off of Jesus and His Word. Fourth, conquer fear through prayer. Philippians 4:6-7 promises God will replace the anxieties you bring to Him in prayer with a peace that surpasses understanding. Finally, fifth, conquer fear by taking a step of faith in the power of His Spirit. Faith is the antithesis of fear (Mk. 4:40). Walk by faith and you'll be fearless. Apply these principles as you continue sharing your faith and you'll undoubtedly grow into the fearless evangelist God has called you to be. Once, after taking then student and current MPM staff member Mark Hodges open air preaching, he told me, "this is the most free I have ever felt in my life!" Crushing your fear of evangelism will do the same for you. My mom is one of the most fearless evangelists I know and she is a testament to the reality that trusting God, rather than living in fear, will result in untold evangelism opportunities!

Rhonda Denison, Master Plan staff member, shares the following story of confronting her lies and crushing her fears: "I love taking college students out sharing our faith. On one such occasion, I was at a campus with two other girls who had never shared their faith before. We started walking around campus and prayed for God to show us who to talk to. And there she was. Wavy hair past her shoulders... a Coach purse... Gucci sunglasses... beautiful... I mean gorgeous. Frantically, my eyes darted around campus; surely there had to be someone else I could talk to! This girl exuded confidence. She would not ever see her need for Jesus, there was no way she would want to talk to us! Silly lie-believing me! There was no one else, so putting on my most confident facade, I uttered these five words, "let's go talk to her!" So we approach this girl (I'll call her Brittany) and one of us asks, "Do you have a few minutes to answer some spiritual interest questions?" And then the strangest thing happened, she said "yes!" Not only did she say yes, she actually went on to tell us how the day before she was talking with her boyfriend saying, "I wish someone would just come up to me and tell me about God." WHAT!? Wow! We shared the gospel with Brittany and with tears streaming down her face, Brittany put her trust in Jesus that day. That day I was challenged in my heart to not decide for someone where their spiritual interest is. I could have walked past Brittany ruling her out, assuming she had it all together. But instead of letting my fear dictate my behavior, I stepped through the fear, and by faith and in the power of the Holy Spirit shared the greatest message on earth with Brittany. Praise God, I now have a new sister in Christ! Luke 19:10 says that Jesus came to seek and to save the lost. Brittany was lost, Jesus sought her out and He saved her!" What an incredible illustration of the importance of trusting Christ and obeying Him instead of being controlled by lies and fear!

Fear and unbelief are learned traits. Baby Christians are usually the boldest and most fearless evangelists; they can't help but talk about their Savior (Matt. 12:34). Chris Bilotta is my favorite example of this. From the day he trusted Christ four years ago until now, he has been one of the most passionate evangelists I know. He loves Jesus and everyone who crosses paths with him hears about it. He is also passionate about encouraging other believers to share their faith. This is normal Christianity. Unfortunately, the fellowship with others that is supposed to strengthen their faith often kills their motivation for evangelism as they internalize the lies their brothers and sisters have come to believe. It is so important to expose the lies that limit evangelism so that they won't multiply unbelief throughout the Body of Christ.

Learn to catch these ten lies, and the others Satan throws at you, before they stop you from sharing your faith. Expose these lies to others when you hear them. I once spoke on these ten lies at a church that was promoting a bunch of emergent garbage, full of these lies. I haven't been invited back but am glad I was able to confront the lies that were keeping that church from all God had for them. Learn to courageously follow your Savior's command to share your faith!

Chapter **3**

Nineteen Relational Evangelism Ideas

"Evangelism is joyfully intoxicating." [10] ***- Earley and Wheeler***

Romans 10:13-14 tells us, "'Everyone who calls on the name of the Lord will be saved.' How, then, can they call on the one they have not believed in? And how can they believe in the one of whom they have not heard? And how can they hear without someone preaching to them?" Effective evangelism requires sharing the Good News of salvation verbally with those we know, love and cross paths with, on a daily basis. We each have numerous opportunities to share the Gospel each day. It is critically important to make the most of these (Col. 4:5). The following ideas will help you creatively bring Christ into the opportunities God gives you every single day. These ideas are so exciting because they will help you be strategic about reaching friends and acquaintances for Christ. As you begin applying these ideas, keep track of which ones you've tried in appendix A and keep notes on what you're learning and how you would tweak these ideas to make them even more effective in appendix B. Also, get notecards to memorize each chapter's main verse in appendix C. Now for the fun part, here are the evangelism ideas sure to revolutionize your life and ministry!

Evangelism Idea # 1 - Meet new people and share the Gospel with them.

Continually meting new people is vitally important if you are going to reach the world for Christ. The second you stop meeting new people your ministry and influence die. Meeting people is the first step in sharing the Gospel. There are a few great ways to meet new people anywhere and anytime. You can share the Gospel with anyone you cross paths with if you'll apply these ideas for meeting people and then work through the sound barriers we'll discuss in the next evangelism idea.

The REACH acronym will remind you of five great ways to meet new people in virtually any context. Even if you aren't an extrovert, you can learn to be good at meeting people (and the Holy Spirit inside you is more than capable). Each part of the REACH acronym is described below.

R - Relate! Smile, compliment, wave, introduce yourself, etc. The longer you wait, the more awkward it will get. Make it a point to be friendly and open with people the second you see them. This will open up countless opportunities for evangelism.

E - Environment! Get out of your comfort zones. Get involved in groups where you will be forced to meet new people (great places to meet people include sporting events, hobbies (Erin's grandmother Barbara often leads people to Christ through her hobby art), classes, ministry events, like concerts, etc.). Look for conversation starters around you wherever you happen to be. Try to begin a conversation based on the person's clothes or possessions (for example, if they're wearing an Alaska T-shirt, ask "Where have you been in Alaska")? Try to begin a conversation based on something from your surroundings (for example, if you're standing in line with someone, ask, "This is quite a line, huh?")? Try to begin a conversation based on something in the media (news, entertainment, sports, politics, etc., are all great conversation starters). Also begin conversations based on shared circumstances (for example, ask, "What movies would you suggest I rent?").

A - Ask questions! People rarely sense others are genuinely interested in them so be genuinely interested in them. Ask lot's of questions. Keep it appropriate. Ask open ended, conversation promoting questions. Refrain from questions with "yes" or "no" answers (for example, asking "What's the best thing on the menu" is much better than asking, "is the food here good?"). Ask good follow up questions to their answers. Ask and then listen!

C - Communicate! Start a conversation by applying the previous concepts (Relate, Environment, Ask). Keep a good conversation flowing comfortably and naturally by asking and talking about their interests, hobbies, goals, background, pursuits, etc. Try to establish common ground. On a side note, always continue learning new things and cultivating new interests so you'll have more areas of common ground with more people. Again, ask good follow up questions to their answers. Stay positive, build bridges and establish common ground. Keep the focus off yourself. Strive to relate with them where they are at.

Finally, **H** - Help! Help someone that needs help or ask for help from a stranger if you need help. Helping someone who needs it and asking someone for help both create natural opportunities to meet new people.

Make sure to remember the following ten principles while you apply the **REACH** acronym! 1) Don't focus on yourself, dominate the conversation or pressure them (give them freedom). If you sense they are uncomfortable let them go. Focus on them (1 Cor. 13:4-8). 2) Don't try to be someone you are not. Be yourself; if you are at ease, it will set them at ease too; if you are confident, it will make the whole conversation go smoothly. 3) Don't be strange or awkward. Smile and be friendly. Exude the fruit of the Spirit (Gal. 5:22-23). 4) Don't play favoritism or set standards for who you will meet and get to know (James 2:1-4). Don't settle in to cliques. Get to know anyone and everyone you can regardless of personal differences. 5) Don't be a quiet, antisocial loaner (Heb. 10:24-25). You can learn to be good at being relatable. 6) Don't stare or invade. Be appropriate with body language and eye contact and respect their personal space and boundaries. 7) Don't laugh at people, awkward situations or topics. Stay positive! Show sympathy and kindness (Rom. 12:15). 8) Don't be wordy or peculiarly silent (awkward silences are always bad). Talk but not too much. Don't hijack a conversation. Definitely don't one-up their stories (even if you share a similar experience, refrain from telling it if it could come across like you're trying to beat their story). Listen and be a good listener. 9) Don't get too deep right off the bat. Russ Akins always says, "Too much too soon too bad; too little too late so sad!" Keep your conversation appropriate. 10) Don't end there. One conversation is just a start. Invite them to something or go along with them if they invite you. Get their contact info so you can reconnect later!

The bottom line: take the initiative in the power of the Holy Spirit! The Great Commission starts with "Go." We can't sit around and wait but must go and meet new people where they are at and then share the Good News with them. Most American churches utilize the sit, wait and hope they show up method. This is a tragic way of blowing the harvest at the most critical time in history to be out harvesting. Don't fall for this American "evangelism" model. Make it a point to take the initiative, meeting people where they are at (just like Jesus did with the Samaritan woman in John 4:1-26).

Evangelism Idea # 2 - Transition any conversation to the Gospel.

Sharing the Gospel involves breaking through four different "sound barriers." This concept was developed by Keith Davy.[11] They are called sound barriers because each involves your need to speak. Each barrier represents a real point in every conversation where you will be tempted to give in to fear and back down. It is vitally important to analyze where you are at in a conversation and trust Jesus and His Spirit in you to cross the next sound barrier. Trusting Him is the foundation. Understand these barriers but go in a context of prayer, filled and controlled by His Spirit. Then, cross each of these barriers by faith!

Sound Barrier #1 – Meeting someone and initiating a conversation. This can be done in a natural way (for example, ask a question like, "What's the best item on this menu?" at a coffee shop or restaurant). After meeting someone, keep asking questions to keep the conversation going. Practice meeting new people and getting conversations going. Use the REACH acronym.

Sound Barrier #2 – Moving from a general conversation to a spiritual conversation. Once you are talking with someone about general topics it is easy to transition to a spiritual conversation by asking thoughtful questions and listening carefully. For example, if you are talking about the news and the bad in the world you could easily ask what their hope is. Keep asking, listening and transitioning general conversations to spiritual conversations.

Sound Barrier #3 – Moving from a spiritual conversation to the Gospel. From a spiritual conversation you can easily transition to the Gospel by asking another transition question like, "what has been your experience with Christianity?" From there it is very easy to continue into a presentation of the Gospel. Make sure to include all the necessary aspects of the Gospel in your presentation.

Sound Barrier #4 – Moving from the Gospel to a decision. No presentation of the Gospel is complete without asking them to respond to Christ's message. Most good tools will include this (For example, Cru's "Know God Personally" booklet concludes principle four by asking the person where they're at and where they'd like to be and then telling them how to get there). Whatever tool or method you use, make sure to convey the fact that they have a decision to make.

Here's a recent example. We were just at a baseball game last week. A young lady came over and said, "you have the most beautiful kids" (yes, your kids are great conversation starters). I said, "thank you" and then asked her where she was from. She said, "Wyoming." I asked her what she was doing in Colorado. She mentioned that she was going to college in Greely. I then mentioned how a friend of mine, Austin Krokos, used to do a college ministry there and asked her if she had ever heard of it. She said, "no." I then asked her what she thought of that kind of stuff. That opened up into a conversation about Jesus. I was simply using the sound barriers concept and making the most of the conversation.

Those are the barriers. They provide a great way to transition any conversation to the Gospel. As you seek to transition your conversations to the Gospel, consider what it is you find yourself talking about most often. Come up with good transition questions for those topics. If you rarely find yourself talking about Jesus, evaluate your heart. Jesus said that the things you talk most about are the things you love the most (Matt. 12:34). If you rarely talk about Jesus, ask Him to give you a greater heart for Him. If you're passionate about Him, no one will be able to stop you from talking about Him.

This concept will help you transition any conversation to the Gospel. Understanding the four sound barriers will also help you evaluate your evangelistic conversations to see where you're falling short (you can evaluate every Gospel presentation by asking yourself how many barriers you got through). Remember not to get duped by the ten evangelism lies. Take a step of faith and trust God to help you transition each conversation to the Gospel! If you practice working through each of these barriers you will quickly find yourself sharing the Gospel fearlessly and often!

Evangelism Idea # 3 - Ask a few good questions.

I'm sure you now see the value of using questions in evangelism. This evangelism idea is simple and really flows out of the last one: get into a spiritual conversation by working through as many of the four sound barriers as you can, focusing on asking questions. If you don't know the person, ask lots of questions to get to know them. Then, ask a direction setting question about what they believe. Be creative, not awkward. For example, if I'm talking about baseball I will mention my favorite team, the Cardinals, and my favorite former Cardinal player, Albert Pujols. I will then mention how I respect him both for his baseball skills and because he is so outspoken about his faith. I will then ask what their perspective on spirituality and faith is. Once you are in a conversation about spirituality, ask them questions about what they believe. After asking the "what" questions ask "why" questions (why do you believe that, etc.) and finally leading questions (if you believe that, then ...). Ask other questions that lead to the Gospel. You'll find most people have no idea what they believe or why they believe it. For that reason, be sensitive and don't crush them; gently lead them towards the Gospel with questions. Two great resources that will help you grow your question asking skills are *Tactics* by

Gregory Koukl and *Questioning Evangelism* by Randy Newman.

Evangelism Idea # 4 - Share Jesus without fear.

William Fay's book, *Share Jesus Without Fear*,[12] describes another great approach to conversational evangelism. He describes five questions which can be introduced to any conversation to transition to the Gospel. Question one is, "Do you have any kind of spiritual beliefs?" Question two is, "To you, who is Jesus Christ?" Question three is, "Do you think there is a heaven or hell?" Question four is "If you died, where would you go?" If they say heaven, you can ask, "why?" Finally, question five is "If what you are believing is not true would you want to know?" These questions provide an easy way for someone to bring any conversation to a spiritual one and an opportunity to introduce Christ and His offer of a gift of salvation to all that put their trust in Him.

Once the conversation has turned in a spiritual direction, seven scriptures can be shared with the hearer. Invite the person to read each out loud from your Bible. Fay uses this technique trusting the power of God's Word to draw people to Him. These verses are Romans 3:23, Romans 6:23, John 3:3, John 14:6, Romans 10:9-11, 2 Corinthians 5:15 and Revelation 3:20. Ask the person you are sharing with what he thinks each verse means after finishing reading it and before continuing to the next verse.

Fay encourages his readers to bring every conversation to a point of decision before concluding and once again, he gives five great questions to help with this. They are: 1) Are you a sinner? 2) Do you want forgiveness of sins? 3) Do you believe Jesus died on the cross for you and rose again? 4) Are you willing to surrender your life to Jesus Christ? 5) Are you ready to invite Jesus into your life and into your heart? These questions help bring a person to a point of decision. If they are ready to put their trust in Christ, you can lead them to do that through prayer. Fay reminds readers to follow up with new believers and there will be more on that in Chapter eleven.

Evangelism Idea #5 - Share a verse.

God's Word is powerful and God's Word always changes peoples' hearts and minds! We often make the mistake of trying to share the Gospel without actually going to Scripture. We can also believe the lie that people won't appreciate Scripture until they know Christ. So here's an evangelism challenge: look for opportunities to share a verse with people you cross paths with! You could share a verse that God has been using in your life or tell a non-Christian friend or co-worker what you've been learning. You could share an encouraging verse with a non-Christian friend or co-worker that is going through a hard time. You could post a verse on Facebook. You could also transition to a verse in conversation with a stranger and see where that leads. I did this the other day and it wasn't awkward at all. I got up to the line at Walmart and saw a gentleman waiting. I asked him, "are you in line?" He said, "no, just looking for my wife." I immediately responded, "I don't know whether you've ever read the Bible but the Bible says he who finds a wife finds a good thing." The man laughed and responded, "well I hope when I find her she doesn't have too much in her cart." At that point the line opened up and, being in a hurry, I had to go. I didn't get to go further in that conversation but realized how easily that fun verse transitioned the conversation to a spiritual conversation! Whether you're bringing up a verse with a stranger, co-worker, neighbor, friend or relative, sharing God's Word with people is always a good way to get into a spiritual conversation!

There used to be a student who would come by the cafeteria (where I do evangelism and discipleship with students), on a weekly basis, to get a random Bible verse from me. Once he asked me for a random verse and the random verse I opened up to had to do with salvation. That led to a conversation about the Gospel and a lot more verses. About a week later another guy I had met a time or two came up and told me, "you remember how you were talking to that other student about receiving Christ last week?" I said, "yes." He continued, "I've always been spiritual and have always watched church services on TV every Sunday but something was always missing. As I eavesdropped on your conversation last week, I realized the thing that was missing was receiving Christ. I had never done what you were talking about so I took that step last week. Thank you for sharing that verse with that other student." Wow! That amazing story would never have happened if I hadn't been applying this idea. So here is the challenge: bring up a verse in some conversation you are having and see where it leads!

Evangelism Idea #6 - Share a verse reference when it comes up.

Master Plan Staff lady Angi Pratt came up with this idea. She was buying dinner once and the total came to $8.38 and was instantly reminded of Romans 8:38-39, "For I am sure that neither death nor life, nor angels nor rulers, nor things present nor things to come, nor powers, nor height nor depth, nor anything else in all creation, will be able to separate us from the love of God in Christ Jesus our Lord." This created an instant opportunity to transition to the Gospel. You can get to the Gospel by asking something like, "$8.38 reminds me of Romans 8:38; Have you ever heard it?" You could do this with all sorts of totals you'll encounter on a daily basis (for example, if your total equals $3.16, you could share John

3:16, if it equalled $2.89, you could share Ephesians 2:8-9, etc.). Remember, ask God for opportunities and pray before you go. As soon as you get the total, just tell the cashier it reminds you of a verse you love and then share the verse.

God's Word tells us it will not return void and our labor in him is not in vain (Is. 55:11, 1 Cor. 15:58). Sharing the very words of God is one of the best ways to get into spiritual conversations and break through the sound barriers. It will also motivate you to memorize more Scripture so you can really be ready at anytime!

Evangelism Idea # 7 - Use someone's name to transition to the Gospel.

What's in a name? An opportunity to share the Gospel! Seriously, every name presents an opportunity for the Gospel. This evangelism idea is so easy and it is a great way to get started working through the sound barriers! Simply ask someone you meet what their name is. Then, quickly, try to think of someone that has influenced you for Christ with that same name. Tell your new friend you have a friend with their same name. Then, continue describing who that friend is and what their influence on you has been. This friend could be a pastor, mentor, encourager or just a friend from church. The bottom line is that as soon as you tell them about this friend and their influence on you, you can begin transitioning into a conversation about Christ by asking what their experience has been with Christianity.

Try tweaking this idea a bit as well. If your kids have biblical names, relate these back to the Gospel in conversations about your kids. If you know the meaning of someone's name, share that and use it as a transition opportunity. Whatever you do, try to make the most of peoples' names, using them as natural transitions to the Gospel.

Evangelism Idea # 8 - Ask about church.

This has got to be one of my all time favorite, easiest imaginable ways to get into evangelistic conversations. It always works. Next time you're out of town, ask someone (at a gas station, hotel, restaurant or wherever you happen to be) what the church scene is like in that city. Whether they're a believer or not, that will instantly begin a conversation about Christianity which can easily be transitioned back to the Gospel. I recently did this while on a trip and had the privilege of leading a guy at a hotel to Christ using this idea! I really hope you get a chance to try it out!

Evangelism Idea # 9 - Ask "how are you?"

My buddy Austin Krokos does this idea a lot and he told me about it. It is so simple and you should try it out today! Ask a simple reciprocating question (one that will likely result in the other person asking you the same thing), "How are you?" They will most likely say, "Good, how about you?" After they ask how you are doing, simply say, "better than I deserve." They will be a bit shocked and will almost for sure ask why you say that (they will wonder if you are some kind of a jerk or criminal). You can simply tell them about the amazing and undeserved grace of God that you have received (Jn. 1:16). This will inevitably open a door for you to share your testimony and the Good News. Be strategic and intentional. Pray and go, in the power of the Holy Spirit, and trust the results to God. Ask the question and then have a blast co-laboring with God (1 Cor. 3:9)!

Evangelism Idea # 10 - Follow up with someone you have shared with.

This idea is very simple yet incredibly important. Most of the people I have led to Christ put their trust in Him sometime after the first time I shared with them. God has undoubtedly been working on peoples' hearts since the time you last shared with them. I encourage you to re-connect with someone you've shared with in the past and ask them some follow up questions. You could ask, "have you thought any more about what we talked about," "have any new questions come to your mind since we last talked" or "what would keep you from putting your trust in Christ?" You could invite this person out for coffee or lunch and talk more about Jesus. We've had students take up to four years of these conversations before trusting Christ. One guy I shared with met with me every week for eight weeks before finally trusting Christ. Keep sharing with those you have shared with before who are still interested; don't miss the often short window of opportunity (remember Jesus' warning in Matt. 13:19).

It usually takes someone six or more times hearing the Gospel before they trust Christ. So find someone you've shared with and try to do some follow-up with that person! If you know of anyone that has trusted Christ recently or if the person you share with does, take the next follow-up step and begin doing some basic discipleship with them. You can get discipleship ideas, resources and tools in my other book *Great Commission Leadership*. Additionally, chapter eleven will discuss more evangelistic follow-up ideas. One last note, nearly every time someone comes to Christ they will be immediately attacked (Satan doesn't like to loose). One guy, that my college freshman roommate Jake Kochenberger and I led to Christ, lost something very important to him and got into a car crash the afternoon after he trusted Christ. He needed to be encouraged that he had made the right decision regardless of opposition. Go ahead and schedule a follow-up appointment with someone you've already shared with; God will do great things!

Evangelism Idea # 11 - Ask someone about their weekend.

This is a super easy, "throwing out the line" idea that you can try this coming Monday. It will work best with people you've never discussed your faith with before. Start out by asking people you see Monday what they did over the weekend. Then listen. When they are done telling you about their weekend, they will probably ask you the same thing. When they do, tell them your weekend was great and mention that you had a great time at church (this is the "throwing out the line" component, pray they bite). You could also mention something other than church as long as you can relate it to God (for example, a retreat, a Christian book you read, etc). Then ask them if they have any kind of background in Christianity or church. You will very likely find yourself in the middle of an interesting spiritual conversation. Look for opportunities to go through the Gospel with them from there.

No matter where they are at with Jesus, invite them to your church next week. This doesn't replace evangelism (you should never do this instead of sharing the Gospel with them) but it is a friendly gesture and you'll be surprised how often people will take you up on it.

The second you ask "what did you do last weekend" you open up a conversation that will quickly and easily go towards the Gospel. As you throw out the line and then continue with your answer when they ask you, you are respectfully giving them an opportunity to "bite." Good chance they will (remember Matt. 4:19, Jesus also used fishing analogies!). I am sure you will have a blast doing this.

Evangelism Idea # 12 - Tell someone how God came through for you.

A few years ago we fought our insurance company for sixteen weeks about payment for our second daughter's delivery. They were legally required to pay the $19,000 bill but initially rejected it. We waited forever for their review, which we finally received, finding it had been denied. I asked our prayer team to pray God would change their minds. Three hours after I sent out that e-mail, I got a call from the main lady overseeing our review; she said she was sorry for overlooking something and said, "disregard the denial we sent you, we have paid this bill." We ended up fighting them for another year and ended up paying a lot of the bill but were still amazed by the miracle God pulled off (we also switched to Samaritan Ministries, a health sharing ministry after that debacle). Bottom line, God came through for us!

That brings me to the next evangelism idea: tell a non-Christian, in your sphere of influence, something amazing your Father has done in your life in the last couple of weeks. Brag on God. Praise Him (praise means declaring His character and acts). He's is your heavenly Father and the source of every good thing you have (James 1:17). Talk freely about what He's done for you and all you have to be thankful for. This will lead to an obvious opportunity for you to bring up the Gospel.

Next time you find yourself in a conversation with someone you want to share with, simply share a story of God's faithfulness and then transition to the Gospel from there. God is constantly blessing you (Jn. 1:16, James 1:17) so talk about it! I hope you have a blast telling others about what God has done in your life and I hope you get to share the Gospel in every one of those conversations.

Evangelism Idea # 13 - Tell someone about the struggles your trusting God with.

Don't hide the hard times you're going through, allow God to use even those for His glory! I've watched Christian friends go through many of the toughest things you could ever imagine, trusting Christ through it all and shining brighter in that darkness than ever before.

Recently, a close friend, George Wood, was diagnosed with a terminal neurodegenerative disease. I messaged his wife, Dianne, to ask her how he was doing. She replied, "We are in a different area of ministry, one of helping people see there is hope in Christ no matter how hopeless your situation may seem in your eyes. Lots of opportunity to share the Gospel and encourage the faint of heart. Kind of exciting but our fleshly desire would never be to be on this journey. 'Not my will but thy will be done,' Christ, our example and our hope." That kind of response, to such a seemingly hopeless situation, is one that will always lead to opportunities for evangelism.

It's been said that you're either in the middle of a crisis, just coming out of a crisis or about to go into a crisis. Why not try this idea instead of getting frustrated the next time you are faced with a crisis (and remember Rom. 8:28 and James 1:2-4). I am sure God will do great things in and through you as you trust Him and I know you'll have tremendous joy while you trust God, allowing

Him to use your trial for His great purposes!

Evangelism Idea # 14 - Transition health complaints to the Gospel.

My friend and accountability partner Austin Krokos relaid the following story: "A grey haired, thick bearded man on my curb was picking up scrap metal in our neighborhood this morning. I helped him lift up some old chain link fence onto his truck, and he complained about how his body is not like it used to be. Then he made another comment about how his body was breaking down. I sensed an opportunity to mention a promise of God's. I asked him if he believed the Bible was true, and he looked at me kind of puzzled. I went on to say that God promises us that when we die, if we know Him, we will be given a brand new glorified body. 'Are you looking forward to that?' I asked. He said 'yes', and told me that he was 'born again' and that he is excited to see Jesus some day. We were able to encourage each other for a few minutes, but I think that this is a simple way to transition into a spiritual conversation when people tend to grumble about their failing bodies."

Great point Austin! Next time you hear someone complaining about health issues, take a minute to encourage them with the hope you have in Jesus. Don't write their issue off, pray for them and share the Good News with them! One guy I led to Christ was diagnosed with testicular cancer shortly after he came to know Jesus. I asked if I could pray for him and if I could ask others to as well. He said, "yes." Shortly after that, he went in to begin treatment and was surprised that there was no cancer whatsoever! God revealed himself to that young man in a very real and personal way that day. Never miss an opportunity to pray for someone's health issues and never forget to share the Gospel with them during those conversations either.

Evangelism Idea # 15 - Transition conversations about the news to the Gospel.

Talking about what's happening in the news is one of the best opportunities you'll have on a regular basis to share the Good News. Whatever the news story might be, follow these tips to begin working through the sound barriers to get to the Gospel.

1) When discussing bad news or a seemingly hopeless situation, ask the person you're talking with what their hope is. That will lead to a conversation about hope and an easy opportunity to share the only true hope.

2) Look for any connections the story has to Christianity or Jesus. Are there Christians involved? Are the issues related to Scripture (does Scripture discuss these types of issues)? Is there Bible prophecy related to this topic? Once you find a connection, bring it up while you discuss the topic.

3) Tell whoever you're talking with that you are praying for this topic or issue. Discuss the significance of prayer and how you've seen God answer prayer. Then, transition to the Gospel.

4) Take a stand on an issue. So much of what is in the news is controversial. When you take a stand on an issue and then relate it to your faith, taking the time to explain why, you'll easily find opportunities to share the Good News as a result. Do this in a loving and sensitive way.

5) Write a letter to the editor about something in the news and share the Gospel with your whole town.

6) You could also post a comment on any news story online and then share the Gospel in that comment.

Those are just a few ways I try to get to the Gospel when I find myself discussing different issues in the news. I know you'll have great evangelistic opportunities when you try this idea out!

Evangelism Idea # 16 - Transition sports conversations to the Gospel.

If you're like me you probably often find yourself talking about sports. I am a die hard baseball and St. Louis Cardinals fan. Transitioning from a conversation about sports to a conversation about Christ is very easy if you'll follow this simple idea. Probably the easiest way to share the Gospel in a conversation about sports is to bring up a Christian athlete in the conversation and then work through the sound barriers. There are quite a few Christian athletes out there so it shouldn't be difficult for you to find one you love! Visit eternityimpact.blogspot.com/2011/03/how-to-share-gospel-in-conversation.html for a list of Christian athletes (and these are just a few of the Christian athletes out there). Just find a few names from that list or any others you know of and Google their name or check Youtube to find their testimonies. Then, bring them up in your next conversation about sports. Discuss how you appreciate their athletic abilities but also their personal stories. Then share their testimonies. From there, ask the person what they think about that and what their background with Christianity is and continue sharing the Good News.

Our nation is obsessed with sports and people always seem to be talking about sports. Why not use those conversations to share your faith? Make it a point to do that from now on.

Evangelism Idea # 17 - Transition movie conversations to the Gospel.

Entertainment permeates most Americans' lives. Many of your friends will see all the major movies that come out so how can you get to the Gospel from a conversation about any of those movies, whether seen in the theater or rented? Simple! Follow these three easy steps.

1) Are there any Christian actors, influences or direct contributors to the movie? If so, mentioning them is a great way to begin transitioning to the Good News. You might think "In Hollywood?" Before you jump to conclusions about the godlessness of Hollywood, think of all the movies released recently that have Christian connections: *Son of God*, *Noah* (as bad as it was it is a great transition to a spiritual conversation), *God's Not Dead*, *Heaven is for Real*, *The Chronicles of Narnia* (you could easily mention C.S. Lewis and why he wrote the series; you could also suggest one of his many classics, like *Mere Christianity*), *The Lord of the Rings* (J.R. Tolkien was a committed believer who actually influenced Lewis for Christ), etc. Each of these present a great opportunity for the Gospel.

2) Are there any themes that are either Christian themes or anti-Christian themes? These are an obvious way to get to the Gospel as well. Whether pro or con, it is easy to say what you liked or didn't like about the movie and to explain why: it either did or didn't jive with your values. You can visit movieministry.com for

more ideas on Christian conversation topics for every new movie.

3) Does the movie address any social, moral or historical issues that you could bring a Christian perspective to? Look for opportunities to discuss your faith when talking about movies with an important message.

Those are just a few ways to get to the Gospel from any movie you happen to be talking about. Of course, you could do these same things in a conversation about TV shows. Finally, before you get burned by a bad movie, go to pluggedin.com to see what's good (and they'll undoubtedly have even more conversation topics in their analysis of each movie).

Evangelism Idea # 18 - Transition music conversations to the Gospel.

Our society is addicted to music! So how can you get to the Gospel from a conversation about music? Simple! Follow these three easy steps.

1) If your favorite band or musician is Christian, share that in a conversation about music. It is a very simple way to bring Christ into the conversation. Back in college, I was a huge punk rock fan and took every opportunity I could, in conversations about music, to bring up some of my favorite Christian punk rock bands. This always opened up into a conversation about Christ!

2) Do the artists or bands in the discussion (Christian or not) have any lyrics that could get back to the Gospel? Mention those, even if they're negative, and then work through the sound barriers. I also used to like the *Smashing Pumpkins* and would often bring up one of their lyrics which said, "Emptiness is loneliness

and loneliness is cleanliness and cleanliness is godliness and God is empty just like me." I would then use that terrible line to ask whoever I was talking to what they thought and then transition to the Gospel from there. Even if the lyrics are terrible, they may still provide a way to bring up the Gospel.

3) Do the artists or bands being discussed address any social, moral or historical issues that you could bring a Christian perspective to? Look for opportunities to discuss your faith when talking about music with an important message.

Those are just a few ways to get to the Gospel from any music you happen to be talking about.

Evangelism Idea # 19 - Transition near death experiences to the Gospel.

I'm talking about dangerous situations when you could have been killed, not the near death experiences some have reported while being clinically dead (but if you have one of those experiences use it to get to the Gospel too). Three of our leadership students were once in a terrible crash in which they could have been killed. One and a half flips in the car and numerous collisions with obstacles could have been the end of any or all of their lives. Not one of them had a scratch, bruise or injury. Praise God! It is so easy to live life with a very natural perspective but these types of experiences jolt us into an eternal perspective. These students ended up sharing this story with many people, pointing to God each time.

Evangelism Is[13] is a great book on evangelism. In it, Dave Wheeler mentions four times people are very open to the Gospel: death (deaths of loved ones or near death experiences), divorce, disease and status changes (new jobs, cities, etc.). Make it a point to transition to the Gospel from stories and conversations concerning these introspection points. Give it a shot, share a near death story with a friend or co-worker and then ask them theirs. Then transition to the Gospel from there.

Go for it!

The relationships and conversations you have were given to you by God for the very purpose of bringing the people you interact with to Him (Acts 17:26-27). As you apply the ideas from this chapter, you'll undoubtedly find yourself enjoying sharing your faith on a daily basis in situations you never imagined sharing your faith in. Remember, you don't have what it takes but the Holy Spirit in you does. Take the initiative, in the power of the Holy Spirit and then trust God to come through in the lives of those you share with!

Chapter **4**

Nine
Servant
Evangelism
Ideas

"Keep to the gospel, then, more and more and more. Give people Christ, and nothing but Christ."[14] - Charles Spurgeon

Serving often opens a great door for evangelism and it is a great way to be intentional about sharing your faith. Jesus tells us, "let your light shine before men, that they may see your good deeds and praise your Father in heaven" (Matt. 5:16). Servant evangelism does just that. It isn't, however, a necessary prerequisite for evangelism! Let me clarify. Christians have often bought into the lie that we must validate the Gospel. That isn't necessary, Christ validated the Gospel at Calvary and He alone changes peoples' hearts today. However, serving others can be one more creative and thoughtful tool you can use for getting to the Gospel. Just make sure that when you do this you also give them Christ! Servant evangelism is a great type of evangelism but it is definitely not the only type and it shouldn't be seen as a prerequisite for evangelism.

Several years ago my wife Erin and our MPM staff friend Laura Krokos were doing trash club, one of our servant evangelism ministries on campus. As they nocked on doors asking students if they could take out their trash, they were quick to share the Gospel with anyone who was interested. One young lady confided in them that she had just returned from the hospital, having been resuscitated from being clinically dead due to alcohol poisoning. She trusted Christ that night. The point of the story is that Erin and Laura were combining serving the students with the Gospel. Had they not been sharing the Gospel it is doubtful whether they ever would have had the chance to share with that young lady.

Servant evangelism does have two unique qualities. First, it is close to God's heart (remember James 1:27). Second, it is a great entry level evangelism technique; you can take kids, new believers and almost anyone to do it and they'll often catch the evangelism bug. With that in mind, this chapter will focus on creative servant evangelism ideas (get even more servant evangelism ideas at servantevangelism.com). Your efforts will be misguided unless you combine your good works with the Gospel so make it a point to share the Good News with those you serve.

Evangelism Idea # 20 - Serve at a local mission or soup kitchen.

This idea is simple and fun. Partner with a local soup kitchen, homeless ministry or other type of service organization. Find a time when you and a few friends, or people from your ministry can come and serve. Schedule it and then plan for a great time. Make it a point to get to know some of the needy people you serve and take the initiative to share the Gospel with them.

Evangelism Idea # 21 - Meet a specific practical or financial need.

Get together with a group of friends and brainstorm through needs you know of. Find a financial or practical need that a non-Christian someone in your group knows has. Then, come up with a solution to their need. That might involve raising money, putting your money together to pay a bill, doing yard work, or something else. Whatever need you decide to meet, do it in the name of Christ, using this as an opportunity to share the Gospel.

We did this for a student once. There was a freshman guy who many of us had witnessed to. He always wore torn up shoes. A bunch of us chipped in and bought him a new pair of shoes. He was absolutely stunned that his Christian friends would do this for him. He trusted Christ shortly after that and ended up spending several years in ministry. He is now in medical school studying to become a missionary doctor.

Evangelism Idea # 22 - Buy a homeless person a meal.

Buying a homeless person a meal will cost you a few bucks and a few minutes, a very small investment that can have a very large impact. Don't just buy them a meal, give them a tract and a Bible and try to share the Gospel with them. Be aware of your situation though, and be careful. A few times that I have done this have turned out a bit interesting. But God can use those situations as well. Once, I was sharing with a homeless guy I had bought lunch for. He wasn't very thankful and began arguing with me and being very awkward in our conversation. Erin, my wife, was watching us from inside the restaurant I had bought him a meal at. While I was talking to the homeless guy, a businessman, in a suit and tie, approached Erin and asked if the homeless guy was bothering me. She explained that I was trying to share the Gospel with him. The man asked her what she meant by that. She went on to share the Gospel with him, leading him to Christ while I was outside. I returned frustrated by my conversation with the homeless man but was thrilled to hear how God had worked through Erin. Never miss an opportunity to share with someone begging for food.

Evangelism Idea # 23 - Organize a help day.

This is an idea which will take a little more work but can have great results. Talk to your pastor and find a time to organize a church help day. You could help single moms, seniors, or anyone that might need it. Then determine how you'll help. You could do a carwash, oil changes, home help (like changing lightbulbs, smoke alarms, or yard work), or meet some other need people may have. Our church once did a trailer park clean up day, followed by a BBQ and prize giveaway for the neighborhood kids. We have also done college "move-in" days, helping freshmen move into their dorms, as well as "trash-club outreach" going door to door taking out students' trash; all of these servant ideas proved to be great transitions to the Gospel. Whatever you decide to do, make sure to include a Gospel presentation.

Christians should be the most helpful people in the world. You've been given so much and there's no reason not to give back. Just make sure to connect your service with your Savior!

Evangelism Idea # 24 - Organize a giveaway.

Everyone likes free stuff! Get together with some friends, or people from your church, then put your money together and figure out something you could buy to give away. Try to do this on a weekend or holiday, when lots of people will be out. Maybe you could do a cooler of ice with soft drinks and water, or candy bars, or snacks. You could even do a free BBQ. It doesn't matter what you get. You should try to buy items that will be appropriate for the time of year you do this (popsicles and soft drinks in the summer, hot chocolate in the fall and winter, etc.). Then, go to a local park or some area where there will be a lot of people. Start giving away all that you bought in the name of Jesus! You could put a little note with a verse or something on all that you give away or just give it away and wait for people to ask why you're doing it. That will give you a great opportunity to relate it to all God has given you, specifically, the free gift of salvation. Definitely take the opportunity to invite the people you meet to church as well.

Evangelism Idea # 25 - Organize a job fair.

There are always people looking for jobs and usually those are the most desperate people who could really use some hope. With that in mind, talk to your pastor and see if you could put together a local job fair. Find churches and local businesses that will partner with you and then plan a day long event. Schedule a few messages on the hope we have in Jesus, along with a few sessions on how to craft a resume, interview for a job, etc. Also make sure that the volunteers who are helping are trained and ready to share the

Gospel one-on-one with people. Provide a free lunch for those that come (either your church could pay for this or you could raise money to cover it). Then, have have a few local businesses hire people on the spot. This will be an effective way of reaching some of the most needy people in your community, helping to meet their physical and spiritual needs.

Evangelism Idea # 26 - Raise money for a cause.

Find a cause that anyone in your community could support. That could be a poverty related issue, disaster relief, a local need (like a community member with health-related financial needs), or something else. Then, get together a team that will raise money for the cause. This will give you a great opening into conversations with people as you meet them trying to raise money. It will give you obvious opportunities to discuss what you are doing and why you are doing it. You could even put together an event that will provide even more opportunities to share the Gospel.

Evangelism Idea # 27 - Go on a mission trip.

I can't think of a better way to get a heart for evangelism than to go on a mission trip. It will rock your world, getting you out of your comfort zones and helping you see the reality of the world around you. It will also, inevitably, give you many opportunities to share your faith, practicing so you'll be ready to do this more once you return home. If you've never been on a mission trip, you owe it to yourself to go, soon! You'll have many opportunities to share your faith and your commitment to witnessing will grow. Start praying today, asking God to lead you towards the trip He wants you to go on. Trust Him to provide for this trip as well, He can do it (visit supportraisingsolutions.org for more info on that).

Evangelism Idea # 28 - Sponsor a child.

Sponsoring a needy child through Worldvision, Compassion International or some other Christian organization is a great way to honor God with your money while building a relationship with a needy child who you can share Jesus with. This will also cultivate a heart for the needy in your family. These organizations have many different ways that you can communicate with the kids you support making it easy to share the Gospel with them. You could even visit them and share Christ with them in person. Most of these Christian organizations will also be sharing with them locally. This is a great way to meet a real physical need and a spiritual one simultaneously.

Go for it!

It is a privilege to serve God and others. Servant evangelism allows you to do both simultaneously. Make servant evangelism a lifestyle; always look for opportunities to serve others. Never divorce service from evangelism. Remember, you don't have what it takes but the Holy Spirit in you does. Take the initiative, in the power of the Holy Spirit and then trust God to come through in the lives of those you share with!

Chapter

5

Nine Day-to-day Evangelism Ideas

"Jesus didn't die to keep us safe. He died to make us dangerous. Faithfulness is not holding the fort. It's storming the gates of hell."[15] - Mark Batterson

You are living in the middle of a spiritual war zone. Your heavenly Father and Commander has placed you on the front lines (2 Tim. 2:3-4). This battle is carried out all around you on a daily basis. Every day you have here on this earth is a gift from God. Scripture tells us, "Each day proclaim the Good News that He saves" (Ps.96:2 NLT). This is a challenge that no true follower of Christ will frown upon. Sure, it's difficult to share our faith every day. But it is not impossible! With a willingness to take a risk and a few good ideas, you can do it! This chapter will help you do just that, giving you numerous ideas for sharing the Gospel throughout the course of any given day.

Evangelism Idea # 29 - Reach your neighbors for Christ.

It is hard to imagine a more obvious mission field than your neighborhood and it is always hard thinking of ways to share your faith with your neighbors. I think my neighbors have been the group of people I have been least effective at reaching out to. Here are eight ways I plan to reach my neighbors for Christ. I hope you get a chance to try some of these as well.

1) Host a pot luck, BBQ or a meal and invite the neighbors over. Play christian music in the background (KLOVE is a good choice) and be intentional about working through the sound barriers.

2) Invite your neighbors to enjoy something special you have that they may not. You might invite them to watch a big game on your big screen TV, swim in your pool, let their kids play in your back yard or borrow your tools. The main idea is to use what God has given you to bless them and then be intentional about sharing the Good News with them as well.

3) Pray for a need they have. Whether it is a health problem, a financial need or something different, ask your neighbors if you can pray for them. This will open up an obvious opportunity to share the Gospel with them.

4) Help them with a need they have. You could water or mow their yard, shovel their snow, volunteer to help with a project they're doing, cover a bill they have, give them a ride or find any number of ways to serve them, opening a door to share with them too.

5) Give them a Christ centered gift for Christmas, birthdays or just for fun. Books and videos are great gift ideas. Try to remember their birthdays and other special days so you can get them cards and gifts on time.

6) Invite them to church. Inviting your neighbors to church will bring up a conversation about Christ regardless of whether or not they come, and maybe they will.

7) Host a Bible study in your home and invite your neighbors. Just make sure it isn't too deep. Keep it Christ-focused, fun and informal.

8) Do a combined garage sale. Do a multi-family garage sale with families from your neighborhood and make the most of your time sitting together all day long.

These eight ways of sharing Christ with your neighbors may just start a little revival in your neighborhood. I hope these ideas encourage you to reach the sphere of influence called your neighborhood, that God has strategically placed you in (Acts 17:26-27)!

Evangelism Idea # 30 - Reach your workplace for Christ.

For many, the workplace is the primary sphere of influence God has sovereignly placed them in to make Him known! It is not a ministry to be shunned but rather a purpose to be embraced. You have an unbelievable opportunity to reach the people you work with every day for Christ. Your daily good attitude and Christlikeness will show them Christ in a way few will ever see (I've heard it said that there are five Gospels, Matthew, Mark, Luke, John and your life and most will never read the first four).

That being said, here are eighteen practical ways to reach your workplace for Jesus. I hope you have a blast trusting God to use you in big ways at the office (or wherever you work) and I really hope these ideas help (several of these will work in your school if you're a student)!

1) Put things on your door, walls or locker that will point to Christ; then be ready to share when people ask. Make sure to change it up every so often to keep the conversations happening. While I was working in the office world I put the *Passion of the Christ* poster up (it was showing then) and it started a ton of conversations.

2) Talk good about your spouse. People will notice and ask why. Seriously, people can hardly believe it when you talk up your spouse and it is a great opportunity to tell them about the reason for your great relationship: Jesus!

3) Communicate your sense of purpose. Every Monday my co-workers would say, "another day another dollar" or something like that. Communicate your passion for serving God both at work and while away and you'll find yourself sharing the reason for that purpose very often.

4) Talk good about your co-workers and boss. Avoiding the workplace gossip mill will speak volumes about your character and bring up opportunities to talk about why you respect those individuals.

5) Pray before your meals. This will get peoples' attention and lead to evangelistic conversations.

6) Walk in integrity, work hard and don't cheat. Don't live a hypocritical life. Once, some of my non-Christian co-workers tried to get me to go to a strip bar. I wouldn't join them and it opened up a great opportunity to share why. Your Christ-like behavior will

definitely point to Jesus, just make sure to speak the Gospel as well (1 Peter 2:12).

7) Serve in your workplace. Replace the water, carpool to work, make coffee, clean messes, carry heavy loads, get the mail, etc. Basically, be the person in your office that does the small things that no one else enjoys doing. It will speak volumes.

8) Start a lunch time Bible study. You could even do an evangelistic Bible study and invite your co-workers to join you.

9) Keep a Bible on your desk or in view wherever you happen to work. While in college, a co-worker at a snowboard shop saw my Bible and began asking about it. She put her trust in Christ, in tears, that night. She then brought her boyfriend to church, introduced him to me and he also became a Christian. Your Bible will open up a ton of conversations.

10) Wear a Christian t-shirt with an evangelistic message on casual Fridays or whenever your job provides an opportunity for that. If that isn't an option, wear a Christian bracelet or something that could spark a conversation. It will open up conversations.

11) Be there to talk when co-workers are going through tough times and situations. Be relatable. Ask how people are doing. Take a genuine interest in their lives. Pray for them. Then, share the hope you have with them.

12) Listen to Christian radio, sermons and audiobooks in the office, car or wherever people will have a chance to overhear you. Good chance they'll ask you about it and be impacted for Christ.

13) Invite your co-workers to church or some other Christian event where they will hear the Gospel.

14) Bring Christ into conversations you're already having at work. Use transition questions to work through the sound barriers to bring conversations about sports, movies, music, news, company situations or other issues back to Christ.

15) Ask how you can pray for your co-workers. This will show them you care and give you an opportunity to share the Good News with them.

16) Brag on God by telling your co-workers what God has done and is doing in your life. Share your testimony with your coworkers.

17) Give evangelistic gifts and cards at Christmas parties, going away parties and other celebrations.

18) Put a verse or Christian quote on the signature portion of your workplace e-mails. People put all sorts of junk in their signatures, why not use yours as an opportunity to share?

If you are willing, God will open up huge opportunities for you to share Christ with your co-workers. My brother Dave and father-in-law Roger are incredible examples of this, they're both constantly sharing their faith with co-workers. Be respectful but do take the initiative! Embrace your workplace as your mission field and have a blast reaching your sphere of influence for Christ!

Evangelism Idea # 31 - Say you're sorry.

We've all had disagreements with people in our spheres of influence. Sometimes we've even hurt non-Christian friends. The natural tendency in those situations is to think we've ruined our opportunity to share Christ with them. Well, not necessarily!

Sometimes telling a non-Christian friend or co-worker you've hurt that you're sorry can open up into an amazing opportunity to share with them. The world is full of pride, arrogance, gossip, slander and running over each other to climb the social latter. When you humble yourself and genuinely apologize, it will get peoples' attention and their entire perspective will likely change. Your vulnerability, humility and kindness will be very attractive. Almost every time I've done this people ask me why I did it. That always opens up an opportunity to share about Christ. Give it a shot, ask the Holy Spirit to remind you of any of your non-Christian friends you've wronged and then try this evangelism idea! Ask their forgiveness and then look for the opportunity to share Christ with them!

Evangelism Idea # 32 - Reach bored people for Christ.

Every time I enter a store or business that looks empty, I wonder how bored these poor employees must be; stuck there for hours on end without any interaction, just waiting for the excitement of some actual work to do, or a person to talk to. I've always thought there must be a way to make the most of the opportunity and share Christ with them. I've tried various approaches but none seemed that great. A new idea finally clicked and I've tried this idea numerous times since. It works!

If you sense the employee in front of you is bored, or if you just realize not much action is going on at the location, simply ask something like, "it looks pretty slow in here, do you ever get bored waiting around?" Almost every time I ask that there is an enthusiastic response as if just bringing up the issue gives them a sense of relief. Usually they say, "yes," followed by descriptions of how unbearable the boredom can be. It is at that point that I say, "I always find a little reading material can help out a ton when I'm bored. Here is a little booklet on how you can have a relationship with God. I hope you get a chance to read it next time you're waiting here with nothing to do. By the way, what is your background with God and spirituality?" So far no one has turned down the tract (make sure you have some on you) and they are usually very happy to talk to you about their background and to engage in a spiritual conversation. This will bring up an opportunity to share the Good News but just be sensitive, they are on the clock so don't get them in trouble.

I hope you never miss an opportunity to share your faith with a bored acquaintance again! And if you're the one that's bored, why not get out and share your faith, it will definitely add some risk, adventure and spice to your life! I hope you get a chance to try this idea out sometime soon.

Evangelism Idea # 33 - Invite someone to church.

This idea is simple and just takes a little initiative: invite people to church! Dr. Thom Rainer says that "82% of the unchurched are at least somewhat likely to attend church if invited."[16] That stat blows my mind! Why aren't we inviting everyone we meet to church? Nobody will kill you for asking. Many students we meet on campus say their families went to church when they were young but quit years ago. I imagine many of the people you find in your sphere of influence are just the same. If you ask them, they'll probably come. Even if they don't, it will bring up a great spiritual conversation (you could ask them what their experience with church has been and transition to the Gospel from there). If they do join you, remember it doesn't end there! After church, don't assume they're good to go. You will need to clarify the Gospel. You could buy them lunch and ask good questions over lunch. You could ask, "What stuck out most to you from the service today," or "What did you think when the pastor said ... ?" These questions will bring up a great conversation and if you are intentional you will be able to share the Gospel with them. Here's a challenge: sit down right now and right out the names of five people you will ask to come with you to church this Sunday. Get more ideas on this at evangelismcoach.org/2010/pray-for-inviting-visitors-to-church and get info on joining other churches for back to church Sunday here: backtochurch.com. Go ahead and start calling, texting or messaging the five people you decided you would invite and trust God to work in their lives!

Evangelism Idea # 34 - Wear a Christian t-shirt.

Christian t-shirts can be a powerful tool whether they result in conversations or not. Your Christian t-shirt will likely be viewed thousands of times before it wears out. They aren't the only conversation starters, nor the best in day to day life, but they are a great tool. They are also awesome conversation starters at work. Before going into full time ministry I worked as the Air Quality Specialist for the Southern Ute Indian Tribe (I monitored air pollution). Pretty much every Friday I would wear a Christian t-shirt to work. People would always ask about my shirts. That resulted in numerous conversations about Christ every time I wore a Christian shirt. From there it was super easy to share the Gospel. Find a few good t-shirts that are thought provoking and sensitive, but not cheesy, that will direct people towards Jesus and lead to spiritual conversations. Then, make the most of those conversations when they come up. On a side note, make sure not to live hypocritically ever, but especially not when you're wearing a Christian shirt. This is one more great way that you can be intentional about sharing your faith daily.

Evangelism Idea # 35 - Buy someone lunch.

This idea comes from Trisha Ramos of *Fish with Trish* (fishwithtrish.com). Next time you're at a drive-through, ask the cashier if you can pay for the car behind you. Then, give the cashier a tract and ask them to give the tract to the next customer along with their free meal, telling them the tract and the meal came from you, the car that had been in front of them. You could also leave a second tract with the cashier. This idea could easily be adapted to a sit-down restaurant as well.

Evangelism Idea # 36 - Tell someone Jesus loves them.

Telling someone that Jesus loves them is a great way to share the Gospel. This works great in situations where you only have a few moments. You could do this at grocery stores as you check out, at gas stations or anywhere else you make a purchase or have a brief encounter with someone. Simply ask, "When was the last time someone told you that Jesus loves you?" Then wait for their response. Whatever they say, make sure to let them know He really does love them. I've had so many interesting responses to this. Once a man told me, "God hates me." That obviously opened up into a great evangelistic conversation. Another time I did this, the lady broke into tears explaining how just a few hours earlier her husband had dropped all of her belongings off at the store and told her not to come home. I was able to share the Gospel with her and she indicated a desire to put her trust in Christ. Another time I did this the clerk told me, "Scram!" That's the only negative response I've ever had though. Go ahead and give it a shot and then look for an opportunity to share the Gospel once you're talking with the person! Even if you don't get to share more, trust God will use the little you did get to communicate to impact them.

Evangelism Idea # 37 - Ask someone if you can pray for them.

Here is another story reported by my friend Austin Krokos, one of the most gifted evangelists I know. He writes, "I was talking to my friend yesterday about money issues. He said he was bummed that he had a dental disease that would cost him $4,000 to fix, but he was in the process of buying a house and could not afford both. I asked 'Wow, can I pray for you right now' He said 'yes' and we bowed our heads for a thirty minute prayer. Afterwards, he said 'thanks, I pray sometimes, but feel like I am asking for too much for myself' I was able to share Scripture with him, specifically times Jesus tells us to ask Him for things. Then I asked if he had 'a relationship with God, or if it was something he was working on?' He said he was 'working on it.' I asked if he was willing to check out a booklet that summarized what a relationship with God began with, He said 'yes.' I was able to share the Gospel with him." Great idea Austin!

I once did this with a self-proclaimed atheist. I asked if I could pray with him and he said yes and I was able to pray with and for him and share the Gospel with him. A short time later he publicly stated that he had put his faith in Christ. This is a great idea and it is so simple. Next time you have an opportunity, ask someone if you can pray for them, then, trust God to give you an opportunity to share the Good News with them.

Go for it!

Every day is a gift. Make it your ambition to live each day with a sense of purpose, striving to share the Good News with those you encounter. Remember, you don't have what it takes but the Holy Spirit in you does. Take the initiative, in the power of the Holy Spirit and then trust God to come through in the lives of those you share with!

Chapter

6

Eleven
Internet
Evangelism
Ideas

"I invite you to consider with me what it would mean for all of us … to spend all of our lives for the sake of all of God's glory in all of the world."[17] - David Platt

This world is easier to reach and hungrier for Jesus than ever before. Jesus said that, "The harvest is plentiful but the workers are few" (Matt. 9:37). That is as true today as ever (visit greatcommission2020.com for proof of that statement). The world is shrinking! Missionaries of past centuries would endure weeks at sea to reach their mission fields. In the early years of the United States, circuit riders would ride thousands of miles on horseback preaching the Gospel. Today, you have the opportunity to reach people from all over the world right from your living room. That's right, you can reach all of the world from your own computer. Although it has contributed an enormous amount of bad to this world, the internet is a tool which can also be used for good. This chapter will focus on several exciting ways that you can reach people all over the world online.

Evangelism Idea # 38 - Share the Gospel in your status updates and tweets.

You can share the Good News with hundreds of people right now! Here's how. Your Facebook status and Twitter tweets are places you can frequently share the Gospel. I'm sure a lot of your Facebook friends and twitter followers are still looking for a relationship with God. Every time you take the initiative to intentionally share your faith in your tweets, on your wall or in your status updates you are opening a door for Christ to work big in peoples' lives. This idea is really simple. Make a short description of the Gospel message your status and leave it there for a while. A few hundred of your friends and relatives who don't yet know Jesus will have an opportunity to hear the Gospel. This idea is a very easy way to expose hundreds of those closest to you to Jesus. Almost every time I post something like this I begin getting numerous comments and further discussions often result.

When you do this, make sure to include all four main points of the Gospel: God's love for them, the sin issue, how Jesus took care of that and finally, what they must do about it. Make sure to highlight that last point as it will most likely start a bunch of discussions. Give it a shot, post a short Gospel message on your social media now. Also, learn more about reaching people through social media in *Reach; How to Use Your Social Media Influence for the Glory of God*[18] by Laura Krokos and Angi Pratt.

The whole world is at your fingertips. Don't waste this incredible opportunity. Use your social media for Jesus!

Evangelism Idea # 39 - Use good evangelism apps.

There are numerous evangelism apps that you can get for free, that will help you share the Gospel confidently. One great app is the Soularium app by Soon Creative. This is the app version of Cru's Soularium tool (there will be more on this in chapter ten). It is simply called Soularium by Soon Creative in the Google play store and *myCRAVINGS i* by Soon Creative in the Apple store. This app is a great conversation starter that will help you begin and transition conversations to the Gospel. You can read instructions on how to use this app in the app after downloading it to your smartphone. Another essential evangelism app is Cru's *God Tools* app. This app includes multiple Gospel presentation conversation tools along with Cru's Holy Spirit booklet and a link to everystudent.com, a site full of apologetics and evangelistic articles and Q&As. This app will equip you to share the Gospel clearly whenever and wherever you happen to be. One more you should download is the *The Story* app. There are others as well. Don't be caught dead without some of these great apps on your phone (or Ipod, Ipad or other devices). Don't just download them and leave them there either. Practice using these tools to meet people and share the Gospel with them.

Evangelism Idea # 40 - Share an evangelistic website.

Here's the simplest idea for sharing your faith you will probably ever hear. Share an evangelistic website with your friends and post it to your social networks. Several ministries focus completely on reaching people through the web. These typically reach thousands daily with the Gospel. So here is the idea: think through any friends you have that don't yet know Jesus and send them a message encouraging them to check out one of the following sites. If the person is a college student send them to everystudent.com (this is geared towards students but this site is good for anyone who might be interested in spiritual things) and send others to lookingforgod.com. Other great links include istheremoretolife.com and viewthestory.com (which allows you to create a customized account and link for your friends). You should also post these links to your Facebook, Twitter or other social media with a short message like, "want to know more about Jesus, click here." If you think these sites are irrelevant, think again; as I write, over 74,000 people today have indicated decisions to trust in Christ on everystudent.com and other Global Media Outreach sites (you can see live stats at greatcommission2020.com). You never know, one of those live decisions for Christ might end up being one of your friends (if you share these evangelistic links that is)! And, in case you were wondering, these decisions aren't just random numbers out in internet land. They are real people and real believers really follow up with them. You could even help with that by visiting globalmediaoutreach.com (that will be the next evangelism idea). Finally, don't forget to pray for these people as you watch these live decisions for Christ and don't forget to share these sites with friends on your networks. Seriously, could evangelism get any simpler?

Evangelism Idea # 41 - Be an online missionary.

Ever wish you could be a part of what God is doing all around the world? You can! God has obviously put you wherever you live to reach people in that area for Him (Acts 17:26-27), but that shouldn't stop you from also being a part of the international revival happening right now!

That's right, God is doing great things all over the globe as we speak. 174,000 people are coming to Christ every single day; that includes 34,000 South Americans, 30,000 Chinese, 25,000 Africans[19] and more than 16,000 Muslims[20] who put their trust in Jesus daily! Again, check out the live stats for Global Media Outreach's evangelism sites at greatcommission2020.com. While those numbers are staggering, those people need follow up and discipleship.

That's where you come in! You can sign up to be an online missionary. Global Media Outreach needs your help! Visit globalmediaoutreach.com and register to become an online missionary. You'll have the opportunity to reach people all over the world for Christ right now! It couldn't get easier than that!

Evangelism Idea # 42 - Share the Gospel with a stranger online right now.

This is another one of Austin Krokos' ideas. Have you ever wished there was a place where you could practice sharing your faith anytime, anywhere and without the risk of looking foolish or turning a friend off to God? Well, there is just such an opportunity. Go to omegle.com for an opportunity to talk with people from all over the world. Be careful using the video option as people can abuse that in crass ways (this is not a Christian site, just a random social networking site). You may even want to just be safe and use the text option. When you go to omegle.com, you will be connected with a stranger somewhere in the world. The first sound barrier will have already been crossed. Apply the conversation principles described in the second evangelism idea in this book as you practice crossing the other three sound barriers, working this conversation around to the Gospel. You will be able to share the

Good News in a very easy and comfortable setting, practicing so that you will become better and better at doing it everywhere else as well. Give it a shot now if you have a few minutes to spare. Remember, never give out personal info on the web, and again, be careful with this site as you never know how people may abuse it. If the person you are sharing with needs more follow up refer them to a good ministry or to one of the evangelistic sites mentioned recently. I hope you have a blast sharing your faith on omegle.com!

Evangelism Idea # 43 - Comment on an online news story.

This idea is simple, easy and very convenient yet it provides an opportunity to reach hundreds, if not thousands, of people in just a few short minutes. Here's the idea: comment on a news story in your local paper that you could transition to the Gospel from.

Good options would be the economy, terrorism, any type of social issue or a host of others. The more controversial the story, the more likely your comments will be read. Be creative and ask God to give you wisdom (James 1:5). Then, read the story, online, and post a comment at the end. You might have to create a login ID or leave your e-mail address but it is well worth it.

Make sure to include a presentation of the Gospel in your post. This is a super easy way to share the Good News with hundreds or even thousands of people in a matter of seconds. Give it a shot! Get online and check out your local news. Then, comment on a story in today's news, transitioning to the Gospel in your comments. You might even relate your comments back to your testimony. This is a simple yet powerful idea that you can do right now.

Evangelism Idea # 44 - Share the Gospel in a Facebook ad.

Sharing your faith with a large number of people has never been easier! One way is to create a Facebook ad. Go to www.facebook.com/ads to get started. Create an ad for your ministry, church, website or blog by clicking the "Create an add" button. You will pay around $1.00 per click on your ad but can set the limit you're willing to pay per day (ex. $10 / day). For every click, there are usually thousands of impressions (people that see your ad but don't click it). That means for every dollar you spend thousands more will get a quick view of the Gospel. Carefully select specific demographic conditions to target your ad to specific audiences (ex. college students in your city). Make sure to use your words carefully, writing your title to portray the big picture of the Gospel in a unique way (for example: Jesus loves you!) and then summarize the Gospel and your link in the next lines. You probably won't be able to afford to run this forever but for a short time period you can reach a large audience with the Gospel and a link to your ministry or an evangelistic website. I hope you try this soon!

MPM Staff lady Laura Krokos put this idea on her blog a while back and one of the readers decided to try it out. He later described running a targeted ad in Bangladesh, India, Nepal, Pakistan and Afghanistan. He set his limit at $12 per day and ran it for just over a month, costing a total of $455. The result: there were around 1.7 million impressions of the ad (so a ton of people saw it), around 10,000 clicked it and watched the Jesus film online (which was linked to the ad), around 6,000 liked it on Facebook, another 475 liked it on the Jesus Film webpage, 370 shared the movie link with their Facebook friends and 100 commented on it. If that doesn't convince you to try this idea out I don't know what will. Give it a shot today!

Evangelism Idea # 45 - Reach people for Christ with a QR code.

You've seen them, the weird, square bar codes on fliers and posters. They're actually called QR codes and they are another way to share the Gospel. You can scan these with a QR code scanning app, which you can get for free in the Itunes app store or Google play. You simply download the app onto your phone, then open it and scan the QR code and it will send you to whatever site the code is linked to. You can generate a QR code for free by typing "QR code generator" into any search engine. Then, find a favorite evangelistic site and create a QR code that will send people to that site (everystudent.com is a great evangelistic site you could use). Then, you could create business cards, fliers, posters to hang up or any number of other creative displays with your QR code. Make sure to include a thought provoking title that will convince people to scan your code. You could even put this on bulletins at your church, telling people that they can learn more about a relationship with Jesus by scanning the code (and yes, there are undoubtedly non-Christians in your church each week). Be creative and think of ways you could use a QR code to spread the Gospel.

Evangelism Idea # 46 - Start a blog.

Anyone can start a blog and it won't even cost you a dime! You can start a blog for free at wordpress.com, blogspot.com or other similar sites. You could write evangelistic, apologetic or other types of posts that would share the Gospel with others. You could also link to other articles, sharing them with your readers. Our friend Laura Krokos started the Missional Women blog a couple years ago and has hundreds and sometimes thousands of reads a day! This is a simple and free idea that anyone could do. Before you start your blog, think of a good name for it and Google a few blogging tips so you have a bit of an idea of what to do and what not to do. Make sure to link your posts on your social media as well. So give it a shot, sign up for a blog today and get blogging for Jesus.

Evangelism Idea # 47 - Put your testimony on Youtube.

Youtube has provided an unparalleled opportunity to reach thousands of people in a very easy way. Many Youtube videos even have millions of views. Go ahead and think of a creative way to describe all God has done in your life, including the main elements of the Gospel, and film it (There will be more information on sharing your testimony in chapter ten and appendix D). If you don't know much about filming or editing, find someone in your sphere of influence who could help (even if they aren't a believer, helping with this project will give them a chance to hear the Gospel). You could even film your testimony on your phone or computer. Then, after filming and editing your video, put it on Youtube.

This idea will help you reach people you've never met before and even some that you know and love dearly. After posting your testimony on Youtube, you can reach more of your friends and family by posting it on your social media as well.

Evangelism Idea # 48 - Post a video online.

Everyone likes watching videos and you can take advantage of that reality for Jesus. We used to do video testimonies on campus and it was amazing how much everyone, even non-Christian students, would focus on the video. Why not use that as an evangelistic tool. Find a video that clearly shares the Gospel and post it on your social media. This could be the Youtube testimony video from the previous evangelism idea or any other video. You could post apologetical videos and debates, encouraging clips from Youtube or Vimeo or any number of other videos that will communicate the Gospel to your social media friends and followers. Take a few minutes right now to search for a good video and post it. You could even make it a point to post an evangelistic video each week!

Go for it!

The internet and your social media have provided you with an opportunity to reach the whole world right from where you are. The Apostle Paul would have gladly given up any limb on his body to have had such opportunities. Commit today to using these tools for evangelism. Remember, you don't have what it takes but the Holy Spirit in you does. Take the initiative, in the power of the Holy Spirit and then trust God to come through in the lives of those you share with!

Chapter 7

Thirteen Unique Evangelism Ideas

"Three-hundred-million years from now, the only thing that will matter is who is in heaven and who is in hell. And if that is the only thing that will matter then, that should be one of our greatest concerns now."[21] - Mark Cahill

With an eternal perspective and a little creativity, you can bring Christ into all the unique things that happen in your life each day. Jesus promised to make His followers fishers of men (Matt. 4:19). Fishermen can't pass a body of water without wanting to fish. Fishers of men won't look at any situation they happen to be in without considering how to make it an evangelistic opportunity. This chapter will help you do just that, describing thirteen unique evangelism ideas. There are obviously countless more but hopefully this just gets you thinking creatively about all the other ways you could bring Christ up in unique ways!

Evangelism Idea # 49 - Write a letter to the editor.

This idea is great because you get to be just like the Samaritan woman who shared with her whole town and saw many people believe in Jesus (Jn. 4:39). The idea is simple: write a letter to the editor of your local newspaper. Just go to your local paper's website and click the letters to the editor link. Start your letter by briefly discussing some story in the news that seems hopeless. Then link that to the story of how Christ found you in a similarly hopeless state and saved you. Make sure to include the Gospel and keep the whole thing concise. You will effectively be sharing your testimony and the Gospel with your whole town (and it will only take a few minutes)! I would love to eventually get to the point where every day someone in our town is doing this. Maybe you could be the catalyst that helps organize something like that in your town. Have a blast sharing the Good News with your whole town today!

Evangelism Idea # 50 - Leave a generous tip.

A friend of mine, pastor Terry Willis, says his goal when he and his family eat out is to tip their servers so much they'll cry tears of joy. That is a great attitude! Unfortunately, Christians are known for being terrible tippers (I have known Christian waitresses who have told me that this is common knowledge in the restaurant industry). Erin and I have always tried to tip our servers more than they would ever expect and we always leave a short message with the tip telling them about Jesus (we usually write it on the receipt). Every time you eat out you have an opportunity to leave a witness for Christ both through giving generously and by leaving a short message. I have had waitresses tell me how much those messages mean to them and have even been able to pray with them before. Also, if you eat out often at a certain location you will soon develop a very good reputation and a very godly witness.

Austin Krokos shares this story: "Before a student leadership meeting at our home when the boys were younger we ordered pizza. The pizza man was coming to deliver, so I encouraged my son Asher to get a Gospel tract to give him with the tip. When Asher went to give him the tract, the pizza guy politely refused. Asher exclaimed in a serious tone 'But you could be in danger!' Finally, the guy took it. Five to ten minutes later, when the college students arrived, we shared the story. We were amazed when they told us that the pizza guy was still reading it in his car as they walked up."

This idea is simple: leave a generous tip (2 Cor. 9:6-15) and then write a simple note about Jesus to your server. Include a tract if you have one. It takes very little on your end but will have results you can't imagine!

Evangelism Idea # 51 - Reach a telemarketer for Christ.

We all hate those annoying telemarketing calls! Our number is on the "do not call" list but we still get calls all the time. Our friend Linn Saunders recently shared a story about how she got to witness to one of these callers. It was amazing! It encouraged me to begin taking advantage of every telemarketing and business call I get. I have since had the opportunity to share with telemarketers from all over the world (since so many companies outsource those jobs). Some of those conversations were with people in countries which can be hostile to Christianity. You might not be able to go through the full Gospel but, whether your getting on-line help, paying a bill or talking to a telemarketer, they are kind of a captive audience. Make sure to make the most of these short but amazing opportunities and share whatever you can in those few minutes. Also be careful to respect their time as their productivity is undoubtedly being monitored. Next time you get one of those "annoying" telemarketing calls think of it as a gift, an opportunity to reach someone for Christ!

Evangelism Idea # 52 - Invite your non-Christian friends to some fun.

This idea is bound to be a lot of fun. Most Christians lose their non-Christian friends shortly after coming to Christ. That's tragic! Brainstorm through your non-Christian friends, even acquaintances from work or other areas, and cultivate those friendships by doing something fun. Plan a day outdoors or some other type of activity and then spend the day hanging out with them. Make it a point to genuinely get to know them. Eat together, laugh together, talk together. Be ready to share the Gospel when that possibility arises but also just make the most of your day together. Don't blow your witness by being a hypocrite. Show them the love of Christ and build a friendship with them.

Do something fun you'll never forget and bring Christ into your fun day as well! This will give you a great opportunity to develop quality new friendships while having a great time in a way that will matter for all of eternity! Give it a shot.

Evangelism Idea # 53 - Share a good book.

We all have non-Christian friends, neighbors, co-workers and relatives we want to share the Good News with. One way to share with them is to give them a good book. Of course, the best book you could ever give them is the Bible. Even if they aren't a believer, you can buy them a high quality gift Bible that would look nice on any bookshelf and would be there the next time they became interested in investigating further. Find a book that would be aimed at their level and likely to answer some of the spiritual questions they have (something like *The Case for Christ*[22] would be a great idea). This would be a great idea for a gift as well. You might want to buy a stash of ten or twenty to keep on hand for whenever you have an opportunity to give one away. I just bought ten copies of *I Don't Have Enough Faith to be an Atheist*[23] to hand out. I hope this simple idea opens up a ton of doors for you to share your faith!

Evangelism Idea # 54 - Share on a bus.

This is a really simple idea. Share on a bus! I was recently riding on my dad's bus and had numerous conversations about Christ and was amazed by the number of people he had been sharing with as well. It is very easy to meet someone by saying "hi" when you or they first get on the bus. From there you can quickly start a conversation and begin transitioning through the sound barriers. Usually, you'll have a captive audience long enough to share your testimony or go through a Gospel presentation. It also seems that many of the people you'll find on the bus will be down and out and seriously needing prayer and encouragement. You'll undoubtedly have opportunities to pray for them as well. This is a super easy way to practice sharing your faith. Just head to the bus station, pray, get on a bus, and go for it; the longer the ride the better!

Evangelism Idea # 55 - Ask an officer for a ticket.

I hope you don't get a chance to apply this idea anytime soon, but just in case you do, be ready. I recently had an opportunity to apply it. This was something I had thought about a while back and told Erin I wanted to do. She told me just not to get a ticket intentionally. Anyway, it happened. Coming back from a day of evangelism on our Crush Fear summer project, I was getting excited listening to the students in my car sharing about all God had done. I didn't even realize I was speeding until I saw the police car pulling me over. The officer asked if I knew why she pulled me over and I said yes. It was at this point that I was able to be very honest with her about how I try to obey the speed limit but often catch myself speeding. I asked her for a ticket, telling her it had been years since I last got a ticket and that I definitely deserved one. She definitely gave me one. All that led to her saying, "we don't meet people as honest as you all that often," which opened up into a conversation about the Gospel.

So, this is an idea you can just hold on to until you next get a ticket. When you do get pulled over, be super honest and bring up the Gospel from there. Again, I hope you don't get a chance to apply this idea anytime soon and encourage you not to disobey traffic laws. I really hope you will apply this simple idea if the opportunity comes up.

Evangelism Idea # 56 - Buy a lottery ticket.

Seriously, this idea really works! I do hope you'll take a gamble on it. I strongly encourage you not to take up gambling of any other sort, including buying lottery tickets, with just this one exception, evangelism idea number fifty-six. This idea came to Austin Krokos and I late one night at a gas station. Purchase a lottery ticket from a cashier and ask him what the current lottery winnings are projected to be. Then ask him how his life would change if he won that much money. Listen to his answer and then give him the ticket and tell him you hope he wins it all (make sure he is legally old enough to play the lottery, that's 18 in most states). Then ask if you can share something else even more valuable with him. He probably won't turn you down. If there is time, go ahead and share the Gospel with him, if not, leave him a tract. Either way, you will have just managed to share the Gospel in a very unique and creative way for just a couple of bucks. Good chance the employee will tell others about the whole thing as well.

Evangelism Idea # 57 - Take a stand.

Taking a stand is often hard but something we're all called to do. When we take a stand for what we believe in it will never go unnoticed. This evangelism idea will scare you a bit but it is worth it: take a public stand for your faith, in a creative and kind way that you can relate back to the Gospel. One great way to do this is to ask a store manager to remove or cover inappropriate magazines. You don't have to be rude but in a kind way you can take a stand. When they ask you why, you can mention your convictions as a believer. This is just one type of stand and there are countless others you could take. If you are careful you will be able to bring Christ into these conversations in thoughtful ways. No matter what happens you will grow.

I hope this idea challenges you and I hope you enjoy the freedom that will result from taking a stand! Remember to be kind and gentle when you do this. Have a blast and remember Samuel's encouragement to Israel, "Even now, take your stand and see this great thing which the LORD will do before your eyes" (1 Sam. 12:16 NASB).

Evangelism Idea # 58 - Host a Q&A.

You wouldn't believe how many students we meet that have been told, by their pastors and youth pastors not to ask "those types of questions." You'd be shocked to hear how many of them were kicked out of youth group because of how they dressed. A lot of these students genuinely wanted to know about Jesus but have been told by the very people, whose job it is to lead them to Christ, that they really shouldn't investigate. I think a lot of that comes from leaders being insecure about their own apologetical abilities. Who cares if you have all the answers? This generation is contemplating relevant life issues and questions and desperately searching for real answers from authentic people. The worst thing you can do is shut them down. God Himself desires that we genuinely seek Him (Jer. 29:13); what a tragedy when we stop people from that. We host Q&A dinners in our home each Thursday and they always provide great opportunities for people to ask real questions and get real answers.

Here's how you can do it too. Get together with a few Christian friends and brainstorm through a list of "seekers" that you could invite to a Q&A. You might also ask your pastor about doing this at the church and advertising it there. Make sure to provide a free meal along with an open, accepting and friendly atmosphere where anyone can come and investigate the claims of Jesus Christ. Have a basket or box along with pens and notepaper for people to write their questions so they can ask them anonymously. Then, after dinner, draw the questions out one by one and discuss them. Make sure to include your guests in the conversation, allowing them to participate as well. I encourage you to allow those in your sphere of influence to make you a little uncomfortable. You may not have all the answers but you can still create a context conducive to exploring who Jesus is and what He says. So here's the idea: invite a bunch of people to a BBQ at your house or at your church and let them ask anything they want and do your best to point to Jesus. You'll be surprised how far this vulnerability goes in establishing credibility with them and sharing the Good News.

Evangelism Idea # 59 - Flash Mob Evangelism.

You've probably heard of flash mobs. Usually they are a form of social artistic expression but why not use this cultural trend as a way to share your faith? All you need is a few crazy friends and a crowded place. We did this with 1,000 college students in Denver, on the sixteenth street mall, on New Year's Eve. It was a blast and we were able to share the Gospel with hundreds of people (and MPM staff Malcolm and Leah Hillewaert, got to lead a guy to Christ!). This idea is fairly simple, but will take some creativity and a willingness to crush your fears. Get a group of friends together. Decide where you're going to go and what you'll do (you could freeze, sing or do something out of the ordinary that will get peoples' attention). Make sure whatever you do is legal. Set your cell phones to vibrate and set all your alarms for the same time.

Then spread out and when your phone goes off, do what you planned. You'll probably get a lot of peoples' attention and that will inevitably result in numerous conversations afterwards. Then, be ready to work through the sound barriers and share the Good News! Who knows, you might even make it into a local paper where you can share even more!

Evangelism Idea # 60 - Invite a few friends to go witnessing after church.

There have been fifty-nine other evangelism ideas so far (and there are forty-one more on the way) so why not put some of those into practice by getting a bunch of church friends together after church to go witnessing? Most Christians never share their faith and most churches are full of those types of Christians. So how about partnering with the Holy Spirit to light a fire in your community? Ask your pastor if he will get on board with the idea. Then, invite people to a short evangelism training (you could teach the SHARE acronym from chapter one) followed by an evangelism time right after church. Provide lunch for them, pick an idea or two from this book (or have a few extra copies to give out, encouraging teams to pick ideas as they go), pray together and then go for it. This simple idea will lead to more evangelism in your town and it will inevitably lead to more people coming to know Jesus!

Teaching others to share their faith is an important part of discipleship and it is imperative, if we are to reach this world for Jesus. In 2003, one of our staff ladies taught a student to share her faith and then encouraged her to witness to her roommate. She did and the roommate put her faith in Jesus! A few weeks afterwards, the new believer was killed in a car crash. Her father got back in touch with his daughter's roommate and lamented how he had been a nominal Christian but had never shared the Gospel with

His family. He asked the roommate if there was any evidence his daughter had known Jesus. She explained how his daughter had trusted Christ before she died. The father, filled with joy, began walking with Jesus and spiritually leading his family after hearing the good news about his daughter's salvation. Teach others to share their faith and you may just experience similar stories. I love Rick Williams' and Ben Renfro's examples of getting their churches out witnessing! Way to go guys.

Evangelism Idea # 61 - Do some garage sale evangelism.

This idea is unbelievably simple and effective. Coordinate a garage sale, get together a bunch of stuff you want to sell and then advertise it in your paper. Invite your neighbors to join you as well (take the initiative to share with them as you spend the day with them). Put out a box or a table with a bunch of Gideon New Testaments, other Bibles and tracts on top of it. Then, put a large note across the front that says, "free Bibles." Ask each customer if you can give them a free Bible (include a good tract with it if they say yes). You'll find very few will turn you down and it will open up evangelistic conversations with many! You'll also make some money on the side which might make this one of the most lucrative evangelism ideas (not that you'd ever do it for that reason!).

Go for it!

These unique ideas will work! There are so many others you could come up with as well. Ask God to give you wisdom about how to reach people for Him in unique new ways and then go for it. Remember, you don't have what it takes but the Holy Spirit in you does. Take the initiative, in the power of the Holy Spirit and then trust God to come through in the lives of those you share with!

Chapter **8**

Nine
Demographic
Evangelism
Ideas

"If they're breathing, they need Jesus."[24] - Mark Cahill

Everyone around you needs Jesus. Fortunately, He is already drawing each of them to Himself (John. 12:32-33). He has sovereignly planned your community in order to best reach everyone in your sphere of influence. Scripture tells us, "From one man He made every nation of men, that they should inhabit the whole earth; and He determined the times set for them and the exact places where they should live. God did this so that men would seek Him and perhaps reach out for Him and find Him" (Acts 17:26-27). Your sphere of influence includes your neighborhood, school, workplace, doctors, dentists, mechanics, electricians, grocers, gas station employees, coffee shop baristas, restaurant servers, and everyone else you cross paths with. God has strategically placed you where you are to reach others for Him. Your community is diverse and becoming more so each day. That demands that you learn to meet different people where they are at, reaching them for Christ (remember 1 Cor. 9:19-23).

God desires to reach every group in your community. If you are sensitive to His Spirit and willing to do a little research, you can find ways to reach these different groups. Here are a few thoughts on reaching various demographics for Christ. The following twelve ideas will help you reach different demographics in your city for Christ. There are undoubtedly more so be creative at reaching those as well.

Evangelism Idea # 62 - Reach kids for Christ.

Many people put their trust in Christ as children (I did), so they are a strategic group to reach. Here are a few great ways to reach children for Christ.

1) Reach your own children for Christ! Make it a point to live out your faith in a way that your kids will see it. Read the Bible with them. Pray with them. Help them experience God at their level and in their unique ways. Involve them in ministry.

2) Reach your nephews, nieces and neighbor kids for Christ. Be a light to the other kids God has put in your life.

3) Get involved in your church's youth ministry. They always need help and you'll be able to reach kids for Christ, impacting them for the rest of their lives.

4) Volunteer for Big Brothers Big Sisters or some other mentoring program.

5) Adopt a child or sign up to foster parent children. Both will involve a sacrifice of time and energy but will enable you to reach these precious children with the love of God.

6) Visit Child Evangelism Fellowship's site (cefonline.com) for more ideas on reaching kids for Jesus!

Don't believe the lie that kids can't make significant decisions. Choose to follow Christ's example of loving and ministering to children at their level (Mk. 10:13-16). A great evangelism tool for sharing the Gospel with kids is the eCube or Evangecube (more on that in evangelism idea #97). Trust God to use you in the lives of the young people around you.

Evangelism Idea # 63 - Reach young adults for Christ.

Remember when you used to be cool, or at least knew what was cool? Skinny Jeans weren't cool when I was in school (and I still don't think they're cool) so I'm beginning to feel like I don't know what the next generation thinks is cool anymore. Being in College ministry, it is often easy to feel a bit clueless about the next generation but these five keys will give you rails to run on when trying to reach them for Christ.

But before we get to the strategy, we must ask, "why reach this generation in the first place?" First, God told you to (remember Mt.28:18-20). Second, no generation in history has had the potential this one does. Transportation, globalization, communication, technology, the internet and social networks have all created our first real opportunity in history to actually fulfill the Great Commission. Third, this is why you are here (Acts 17:26-27). The harvest is so ripe, the problem isn't with the harvest but rather with the lack of harvesters (remember Mt.9:36-38). It is time we begin working to reach the next generation for Jesus. Here's how you can do it. Reach today's young adults by following these five keys:

1) Be real, authentic and vulnerable. This generation is searching for leaders that will be honest with them, showing them what it really looks like to walk with Christ. Don't sugar coat things to portray an image that isn't true.

2) Make things relevant to them. This generation expects our presentation to be relevant (but don't compromise the truth). Don't burden them with formalities, programs that have worked in the past or King James English. Meet them where they are at, helping them understand and apply God's Word in their lives and situations. Share the Gospel with them boldly and personally. Hear out their questions. Help them find answers.

3) Be relational. This generation demands that ministry be relational (and that's a good thing!). As much as they emphasize relationships, true relationships are harder than ever to find. So really invest your life in them, not just inviting them to meetings and events you want them to come to.

4) Invite them to be a part of a revolutionary cause (there is no greater revolutionary cause than the Great Commission). This generation wants to change things, to make a difference. That has often resulted in working for the wrong types of change but that's water under the bridge. Help those you minister to be a part of changing things for Jesus (not just sitting around talking about it).

5) Give them a Role in the process. This generation yearns to have a role in what is happening. The days of churches filled with spectators are coming to an end as the spectators die off. This generation is unwilling to sit on the sidelines so give them a role in all God is doing.

Those are just a few ideas. Having been in college ministry for more than a decade I can assure you they work!

Evangelism Idea # 64 - Reach senior citizens for Christ.

Never believe the lie that seniors are stuck in their ways and will never come to know Christ. My grandmother put her trust in Christ the day before she died. Many seniors, confronted with the reality that their time here is becoming shorter and shorter, are undoubtedly thinking more about spiritual things than ever before. Make it a point to reach out to them for Christ. Here are five ways you can do that.

1) Help seniors with house and yard work. I'm sure there are older neighbors in your neighborhood that could use some help around the house. They may not ask you but probably wouldn't turn you down either. Help them out and use that as an opportunity to share the Good News with them.

2) Give them rides. Some of your older neighbors, friends and acquaintances may be unable to drive and may need rides to appointments. Volunteer to help them.

3) Help an elderly person at the grocery store. Just yesterday I ran into a lady that couldn't get a large bag of dog food into her cart and I was able to ask if I could help. Why not look for opportunities to help when you're shopping.

4) Coordinate a retirement or nursing home outreach. Most elderly people love meeting young faces and often enjoy simple activities you can organize. We recently brought a group of college students to a low income nursing home. We sang with the residents, played bingo with them, gave them prizes and just got to know

them. It provided a great door for spiritual conversations.

5) Spend time with them. You could take them out to dinner, drop cookies off and spend a few minutes chatting or something else. Just make it a point to cultivate a friendship with elderly people in your sphere of influence, seeking to reach them for Christ.

Whatever you do, don't miss opportunities to share the Gospel with the senior citizens you know. Genuinely love them and take the initiative to share with them.

Evangelism Idea # 65 - Reach atheists for Christ.

All of us have atheist friends. Most of my atheist friends are too smart to flat out call themselves atheists (they recognize the logical fallacy; it is logically impossible to make an absolute negation) so they say they are philosophical agnostics but practicing atheists. That doesn't seem any better to me. If atheism is a logical fallacy why should living your life according to a logical fallacy be any smarter than stating the fallacy in the first place? Regardless, I have nothing but the highest respect for many of these atheist friends. There are always some that lack intellectual integrity and are belligerent in their discussion of these issues but more often than not, I find them to be fun, thought provoking and interesting people that I consider friends. Here are a few pointers I would suggest for all of you that want to reach out to your atheist friends.

1) Take the initiative and don't freak out! You're faith isn't based on a leap but rather on a confident step. There is a foundation of logic, empirical data, evidence and history that make your position the most logical position. If your atheist friend is reasonable, they will have to be open to the evidence, if they are

not, if they are ideologically motivated, you won't change their mind. Either way, all you need to do is confidently share the evidence, live what you preach (hypocrites turn everyone off, including atheists) and be aware of smokescreens. I've often found that atheists claim to be so as a smokescreen. Just take the initiative to engage your atheist friend in discussion. Ask them out to coffee and a discussion or give them a book reading challenge (there are so many good books you could suggest, a good bet would be *I Don't Have Enough Faith to be an Atheist*[25] by Geisler and Turek). Whatever you do, don't cower in the corner of Christian insecurity, take the initiative to discuss the issues.

2) **Know what you're talking about.** As a Christian, I'm often embarrassed by the weak and unintelligent answers many Christians give in discussions with atheists. If you're going into a discussion of this type please, know what you're talking about or at least be committed to learning. A great place to start is thebestfacts.com.

3) **Base your argument on data and logic.** Don't be afraid of science. Don't fall into the "The Bible is true because it says so" trap. That only works if they already believe the Bible and they don't so don't take that approach. Atheists have tried, without success, for hundreds of years to destroy the Christian faith. They haven't managed to. The arguments are solidly in your favor; know them and share them with atheist friends. Give them evidence. Avoid "Christianese," (don't use Christian words they won't be familiar with). Get familiar with solid logical arguments for God's existence, like the cosmological argument, the teleological argument, the moral argument and others. Finally, make them use data and logic too. Don't tolerate the atheist's favorite trick, the *Ad Hominem* attack (or any other logical fallacies they like to use).

4) **Use statistics and don't let them get out of stats.** I love sharing statistics when I can. For example, statistics show the impossibility of chemical evolution and the formation of the first

cell out of a primordial soup. Just make sure your statistics are legitimate (so do your homework!).

5) Talk about the Big Bang! As believers, we definitely don't believe in a naturalistic view of the origin of the universe. Unfortunately, most Christians are unaware that physics has proven that the universe began out of nothing a finite time ago. That is what scientists refer to as the Big Bang and it is incredible evidence of creation. You don't have to agree with all the implications of Big Bang cosmology but don't throw out this wonderful opportunity to point back to creation.

6) Don't forget history and archeology. Whether you're discussing Christ's resurrection, the reliability of the Bible or various other apologetical topics, the Bible and its claims are supported by history. Learn your stuff and be ready to defend your faith from a historical perspective.

7) Call them out on their "autophagic" (self-destructing) statements. If they say there is no absolute truth, ask them if that statement is true. If so its false and if not is false. The statement is self destructive. There are many more just like that that atheists often use. Always ask if their statement can apply to itself.

8) Discuss moral objectivity. They know right from wrong. Put them on the spot. C.S. Lewis and other famous atheists have come to faith in God because of the moral argument for God's existence. Learn how to defend this argument and use it. Appeal to their knowledge of right and wrong in your defense of your faith.

9) Ask lots of questions. Don't give them an intellectual free pass. Don't let them off the hook! Be nice but go after them. Ask questions that will put them on the defensive. Ask them what evidence leads them to atheism. There's no good evidence for atheism but they've probably never considered that. Don't interrupt (give them enough rope to hang themselves so to say). Too often, Christians are always on the defensive; turn the tables a bit.

10) Keep the discussion going and going in the right direction. Give them good books to read. Don't presume to know everything (study your apologetics). Love them. Don't take offense at their disparaging comments about God (they might say and do crass things just to get a rise out of you; don't patronize them). Pray for them. Finally, keep the discussion focused on the main issue: Jesus! He alone has the answers and He alone is working in your friend's heart (that's usually more of an issue than their intellect). Trust Him. Do your best to love your friend and don't back down from sharing the only Good News!

Don't back down from apologetical conversations with atheists. My friend Justin Wynne is a great example of this. Don't perpetuate the lie that Christians are mindless. I once saw a sign in front of a church that read, "faith sees God, intellect does not." What garbage! God has called you to love Him with all your mind so do that (Mk. 12:30)! Again, please check out thebestfacts.com and memorize our apologetics acronym. It will equip you to thrive in these types of discussions. Also, go to godsolutionshow.com and listen to all my archived apologetical radio show MP3s. Finally, carm.org is a great resource for any apologetical questions you may have. These resources will equip you with solid answers for your apologetical conversations. Remember, the main point of apologetics is evangelism, so don't get proud about all you learn and know, rather, use it to reach people for Christ.

Evangelism Idea # 66 - Reach homosexuals for Christ.

I am by no means an expert on this subject but working with college students we find there are students struggling with homosexuality and same-sex attraction in our ministry pretty much every year. They often come to us asking for answers. It is important to remember that sin is sin and we should never look down on them thinking their sin is worse than other peoples' sin. We should love them with open arms the same way Christ has loved us.

Here are a few key points for sharing your faith with gay and lesbian friends you know (these come from a former ministry to homosexuals):

1) See them as people not as homosexuals.

2) Be willing to listen to them and build friendships with them.

3) Point your friend to Jesus not heterosexuality. They need Jesus first. Trust Jesus to work in their lives once they have trusted in Him.

4) Don't expect to know all the answers. Be willing to learn about this topic. I suggest reading books by Mike Haley and learn more by visiting desertstream.org or bradycone.com.

5) Give them hope for something better. Jesus offered the abundant life and that comes through following Him and obeying His Word. Failing to do that results in untold pain. Help them realize that Jesus offers more than any sexual lifestyle ever could. Another great way to share this hope with them would be to share a testimony of a Christian who left homosexuality with them. You could share Mike Haley's testimony, Brady Cone's testimony (you can find that at godsolutionshow.com) or some other testimony.

More important than anything though is to genuinely love them. They need to know you accept and love them as people. In that context of authentic love you can share the hope we have in Jesus with them.

Evangelism Idea # 67 - Reach Mormons and Jehovah's Witnesses for Christ.

Mormons and Jehovah's Witnesses are growing cults that have recently been thrust into the limelight (especially with Romney's presidential run). Many Mormons and Jehovah's Witnesses have perpetuated the lie that they are just denominations of Christianity. That is not true so don't believe it. Here are six easy ways that you can reach Mormons and Jehovah's Witnesses for Christ.

1) Live a transparent life of obedience to Christ. Mormons and Jehovah's Witnesses are very strict and legalistic. Don't let your personal sin burn your credibility with them. Make it a point to explain grace to them.

2) Take the initiative. Don't just assume that since they believe in Jesus they're fine. They believe in a very false picture of Jesus and they do not teach the way to salvation in Christ. Set up an appointment to discuss these issues with Mormon and Jehovah's Witness friends and be ready to invite their missionaries into your home when they come knocking. Do your homework and know how to challenge their beliefs (but do this in love).

3) Learn relevant apologetics. The historical and scientific evidence against Mormonism and the Jehovah's Witnesses is absolutely overwhelming. The errors in the *Book of Mormon* are staggering and the Jehovah's Witnesses have changed the Bible hundreds of times (their "version" is the New World Translation). Learn some of these issues and be ready to gently discuss them with Mormons and Jehovah's Witnesses you meet, know and love. You can learn some of these apologetical issues at godsolutionshow.com (check out the shows on Momonism, the

Trinity and the deity of Christ). You can also find more information at saintsalive.com and carm.org. Be prepared as they will often build their case using Scripture taken out of context in seemingly convincing ways.

4) Explain why feelings aren't enough. Mormons, in particular, believe that truth is confirmed through a "burning in the bosom" emotional experience. Make sure to explain why emotions can lead you in good and bad directions. Explain the difference between faith based on facts and emotions based on circumstances.

5) Focus on the Gospel. Although they may say they believe salvation is by grace through faith, they maintain that works are necessary for salvation. Neither Mormons nor Jehovah's Witnesses believe that Jesus is who the Bible says He is. Salvation is found in no one else (Jn. 14:6, Acts 4:12, 1 Jn. 5:12) so make sure to clarify who Jesus really is. Make sure to take every conversation you have with them back to Jesus and the Gospel.

6) Keep following up with them. It is doubtful your Mormon and Jehovah's Witness friends will leave their false worldviews behind after one appointment. Don't assume the opportunity is lost. Trust God to continue working in their lives after you talk with them and keep praying for them and following up with them.

Make it a point to reach the Mormons and Jehovah's Witnesses you know and the ones God brings into your life for Jesus. They are genuinely interested in Jesus so don't miss the opportunity to share Him with them. Be prepared and learn some basic apologetics for these conversations so you'll be ready when they come to you (and because of their evangelistic natures that will likely be frequently). Finally, as we talk about evangelism, learn something from these groups. They are some of the most active evangelists on the planet. We should be even more committed to sharing the real Gospel with people!

Evangelism Idea # 68 - Reach Muslims for Christ.

Islam is the second largest religion in the world (after Christianity). Most Muslims were born into Islam and very few converted to it. Even fewer have ever heard reasons for or against Islam or any other faiths. They also have a high view of Jesus and a deep interest in spiritual things. For those reasons, don't ever miss an opportunity to cultivate relationships with Muslims and don't ever neglect to share the Gospel with them. Here are seven proven ways that you can reach Muslims for Christ.

1) Live a transparent life of obedience to Christ. Islam is a strict religion of rules and regulations. Don't let your personal sin or freedom in Christ burn your credibility with them. When you are with them, stay away from behavior that you're fine with but that they will be very uncomfortable with (for example, eating pork).

2) Build friendships with them. Be ready to share Christ with Muslims every time you can but also be willing to grow close friendships with them, knowing Muslim cultures are usually collectivistic and friendship oriented. You naturally share many common values so develop friendships with them based on those shared values. Then, take the initiative to bring Christ into those friendships.

3) Know your apologetics. Again, carm.org is a great resource for apologetics for your conversations with Muslims. There are also numerous good books you could read (check out *Seeking Allah, Finding Jesus*[26] by Nabeel Qureshi). Make sure to focus first and foremost on the evidence for your Christian faith, the reliability of the Bible and the historicity of the Christian view of Jesus. Build the case for your faith rather than belittling theirs.

Definitely refrain from speaking badly of Mohammed. This will turn them off quicker than anything you could ever do. In stead, speak highly of Jesus, using their high view of Him as a transition point.

4) Read the Quran and respect the Bible. Muslims respect the Quran so much that they always place it on the highest shelf in the house and they never lower it below their waste when holding it. Reading the Quran will tell you a lot about them and it will show them you respect them and their beliefs. Don't ever belittle the Quran to them, rather share apologetics in a gentle way. Show them that you respect your Bible as much as they respect the Quran and let them read it as well.

5) Focus on the Gospel. Most Muslims that I have witnessed to are convinced they are going to hell. Most of them readily admit that they could never fulfill all the requirements of their faith. That is a very hopeless conundrum so share the hope you have with them.

6) Ask your Muslim friends how you can pray for them and then pray for them! You should always pray for those you're witnessing to and you should definitely let the Muslims you love know that you are praying for them. It will show them that you care.

7) Keep developing relationships with them over time. Follow up with them often, inviting them into your home and family. Share good books and resources with them. Pray for them. Trust God to work in their lives.

Again, Muslims have a high view of Jesus and are spiritually interested (remember, a Muslim source even admits 16,000 Muslims put their trust in Christ each day[27]). Don't let your fears or insecurities keep you from reaching them for Jesus. Make it a point to share your faith boldly and lovingly with Muslims you meet, know and love.

Evangelism Idea # 69 - Reach Jewish friends for Christ.

There are several million Jews living in the United States and you likely have Jewish friends, neighbors, co-workers and acquaintances. Consider it a privilege to be able to share the Gospel with God's own chosen people! Here are a few ways to do that.

1) Ask if they practice their faith. Most do not and of those that do, there are many different categories. Get to know what they really believe and then study up on that so you'll be better prepared to talk with them later.

2) Share Messianic prophecies with them. Most Jews are not very familiar with Jesus' fulfillment of more than one-hundred Messianic prophecies (find some of those at godsolutionshow.com). Familiarize yourself with a few Messianic prophecies and set up a time to get coffee with a Jewish friend and go over them together.

3) Prepare to deal with Jewish objections to Jesus. Research some of the Jewish objections to Jesus and be ready to answer those questions when they arise.

4) Apologize for the church's past anti-semitism. The church has done many horrible things to the Jews throughout history. You can and should apologize for this terrible past, making sure to clarify God's love for His people.

5) Stand with Israel today. Israel is probably the most hated country on this planet, and unjustly so. They comprise an infinitesimally small percentage of the Middle East, they have historical roots there which are unmatched by anyone, and they are the most persecuted people group in the history of the world. They

are being attacked by terrorists on a daily basis. It is unbelievable how they, after all of this, are constantly maligned. With that in mind, stand with the nation of Israel and let your support of the Jewish people create opportunities for the Gospel.

6) Clarify the Gospel. Practicing Jews will be overwhelmed by their inability to fulfill all the requirements of the law and non-practicing Jews need to hear the Gospel as much as anyone. Don't neglect to share the Good News of Jesus Christ with Jews you know or meet.

Some day, all of Israel, God's chosen people, will be saved (Rom. 11:26). Get excited that you get to be a part of fulfilling that prophecy by sharing your faith with the Jewish people God brings into your life.

Evangelism Idea # 70 - Reach people from Eastern religions for Christ.

There is no way I could go into detail concerning every Eastern religion in this short evangelism idea. Instead, I will try to give a few common themes that run throughout some of the major Eastern religions and share a few ideas for reaching people from these different belief systems. Indian religions (like Hinduism, Buddhism, Jainism and Sikhism) and Asian religions (like Taoism, Shintoism and Confucianism) are polytheistic, pantheistic, panentheistic and animistic religions; none of them are monotheistic like Christianity. Indian religions share themes of *karma*, meditation, reincarnation and becoming one with the universe while Asian religions share themes of living in harmony with nature and the universe, family duty, ancestor worship and humane, ordered conduct. Modern Western evolutions of these faiths have resulted in an untold number of vague spiritual belief systems that are as diverse as the people holding them. Reaching people from these backgrounds can be difficult but there is no reason you shouldn't trust God to use you in their lives. Here are a few simple ways to reach out to these people.

1) Befriend people from these religions and get to know them. Most of these cultures value relationships and will respect your desire to build friendships with them.

2) Ask them about their religion. Most of us are somewhat clueless about many of these Eastern religions, so why not ask your friends who follow these religions what they're actually following? Let them explain their views to you and be diligent to really listen and get to know them and what they believe. This is especially important when discussing these issues with Westerners who believe their own hodge-podge of Eastern religious ideas. For example, if your friend says, "I'm a Buddhist," ask them what type of Buddhism they follow (there are very few Westerners I've asked this of who even knew how to answer). Draw your friend out so you know exactly where they are coming from.

3) Study up on your own. A great resource that describes each of these faiths in detail is *The Popular Encyclopedia of Apologetics*.[28] Make it a point to learn more about your friends' religious beliefs so you can continue talking with them.

4) Lovingly discuss the issues with their faith. For example, you may point out the logical impossibility of reincarnation. You can summarize this with three main points. First, Pantheism has no standard of right and wrong so how can anything be considered evil? Second, how did reincarnation begin? In other words, where did evil come from in the first place? They usually assert that there have been an infinite number of lives before this one, which is an infinite regress, which is a logical fallacy. Finally, third, if the universe is eternal, like they claim, why hasn't reincarnation achieved perfection. Again, find out more on this in *The Popular Encyclopedia of Apologetics* and sensitively discuss what you learn with

your friends.

5) Look for transition points. A friend of mine and I were able to lead a young man, Dharma, to Christ in Nepal. We did this by initiating a conversation and friendship with him and then discussing Christian holidays and Hindu holidays. As we discussed similarities and differences, we were able to share the Gospel. This young man came to see Jesus as his only hope of escape from the horror of reincarnation (it does not have the appeal there that it does here).

6) Clarify the sin issue. This is important in all evangelistic conversations but especially here. Indian religions believe in *Karma* and the reality that all of our personal wrong must eventually be paid for. Asian religions believe in the importance of living within the natural order of the universe. All of these Eastern religions recognize that things aren't the way they should be. This is a great transition point to the issue of sin. If they don't understand sin, explain the harmful results of human selfishness and the need for forgiveness in order to achieve reconciliation.

7) Give them a good book. Many of Ravi Zacharias' books would be great suggestions for people who follow Eastern religions (I've bought his book *The Lotus and The Cross*[29] for Buddhist friends). Then, meet up to discuss the book with them afterwards.

8) Focus on Jesus and the Gospel. Jesus has real answers that Eastern religions are void of. Don't shy away from the Gospel. Be respectful of their differences but don't refrain from sharing the truth of the Gospel with your friends. Just like my friend Dharma, who trusted Christ, your friends are probably acutely aware of the hopelessness of their faiths. Share the hope you have in Jesus with them.

Like I said earlier, these belief systems are diverse and can't just be piled into a single category. Study these faiths and prepare for opportunities to share the Gospel with friends who have embraced Eastern religions.

Go for it!

This section has focused on a few ideas for reaching different demographics for Christ. It was not meant to be exhaustive (nor could it be). There are so many other religions, cults, worldviews and demographic categories that you'll encounter. Make it your mission to be prepared to share your faith with all of these. Study up on your apologetics but don't let that take the place of simple, Spirit-filled evangelism. Everyone needs Jesus, the harvest is ripe (Matt. 9:37) and the whole world needs to hear the Gospel (Rom. 10:13-15). Lovingly share your faith with everyone you meet, regardless of how different they are from you. Remember, you don't have what it takes but the Holy Spirit in you does. Take the initiative, in the power of the Holy Spirit and then trust God to come through in the lives of those you share with!

Chapter

9

Sixteen
Holiday
Evangelism
Ideas

"I ask you to please recognize now how much influence
you can have, before you have a chance to get consumed
with materialism."[30] - Hershey and Weimer

It is easy to get settled into the comfortable American dream, thinking that life is all about being happy. That can affect the way we view the holidays. We can believe the lie that holidays are holidays from work and from ministry. Don't believe that for a second. Don't get sucked into the materialism that epitomizes holidays for so many. Recognize that holidays, especially those with a Christian history, are opportunities to share the Good News. God's Word commands us to "make the most of every opportunity" (Col. 4:5). It's easy to let holidays come and go without making a point to witness to anyone. Don't ever make that mistake again! Follow these holiday evangelism ideas to get the ball rolling and come up with your own ideas for holidays not listed here.

Evangelism Idea # 71 - How to share your faith during New Year's celebrations.

Each new year brings excitement and anticipation about the future. Make the most of that by following these five New Year's evangelism tips.

1) Go out witnessing one last time! Close out the year by doing some evangelism on December 31st. You'll never be able to witness that year again (just like you won't be able to witness in heaven), so make the most of the end of the year.

2) On New Year's Eve, go out, instead of staying home, and meet some new people. Work through the sound barriers and ask them how the previous year panned out for them. Mention how God was faithful to you over the past year and use the occasion to share the Gospel.

3) On New Year's Day, ask people what their hope for the new year is and then share your hope in Jesus with them.

4) Everyone wants to start the year off right and many people will be making lists of resolutions (which, unfortunately, usually last only a week or two). Ask someone what their New Year's resolutions are and then be ready to share yours. Make sure one of yours is to know and love God better in the coming year. Sharing that will intro into a great conversation about the Gospel.

5) Put a New Year's status update on Facebook or tweet a New Year's message pointing people to Jesus.

Those are just a few ideas but I hope they help you make the most of each new year!

Evangelism Idea # 72 - How to share your faith on MLK Day.

Martin Luther King Jr. Day is a great time to share your faith! As you talk with friends, classmates, co-workers and people you cross paths with on MLK Day, ask a few questions and then transition to the Gospel.

The first question could be, "What is your dream?" This might catch people off guard but it will open up an interesting conversation. A second question you could ask might be, "If MLK was alive today, what would he be fighting for?" You might also ask why they think he did what he did and what motivated him. You could bring up his own words to help answer that question; he said "I just want to do God's will." Once you ask these questions and begin a conversation, work through the sound barriers. To get through the sound barriers, you might use some of MLK's other quotes. So many of his quotes mentioned God so Google his quotes before leaving to share your faith and have a few ready for your conversations.

Evangelism Idea # 73 - How to share your faith during the Superbowl.

It might not be an official holiday but it's definitely celebrated here in the U. S. Almost everyone loves the Superbowl. The following five ideas for sharing your faith on Superbowl Sunday are bound to work.

1) Party! You could either have people over or join them elsewhere (you may meet more new people by going to someone else's party). Wherever you end up, the more people you're with, the more opportunities you'll have. Transition your conversations with these people to the Gospel.

2) Share football testimonies. You could share Tony Dungy's *I am Second* testimony or many others. Just search for these on Youtube before the party and be ready to share them if the opportunity arises. This past year, we were devastated by the Broncos loss to the Seahawks, but, as people began heading for the door before the game ended, I asked if we could play a quick interview to put things in perspective. We played Mark Driscol's interview with the Seahawks, including their statements that Jesus is better than the Superbowl.

3) Be ready to start a conversation based on any commercial you see that could transition to the Gospel.

4) Ask people what they think of an outspoken Christian football player or someone who is outspoken for another religion or cause. Then, transition the conversation to the Gospel.

5) Put evangelistic, Super-bowl related comments on your social media.

Whatever you do on Superbowl Sunday, ask God for opportunities and then be ready to share the Good News! This may not be an official American holiday but it is sure celebrated as one. Some of these unique ways of sharing Christ on Superbowl Sunday will equip you to score a touchdown in the Superbowl of eternity. That will lead to a party in heaven that will blow the greatest Superbowl party ever thrown out of the water (Lk. 15:7). Seriously, start planning now so you can make the next Superbowl the best ever!

Evangelism Idea # 74 - How to share your faith on Valentine's Day.

What better day to share your faith in God, Who is love (1 Jn. 4:16) than the day our society celebrates love. Here are a few ideas for sharing your faith on Valentine's Day.

1) Do a Valentine's Day survey. Ask people how they define love. Then, use that as a way to transition to the Gospel.

2) Tell people that God loves them, then share with them as opportunities arise.

3) Give out Valentine's candy with verses about God's love attached. Doing this brought up an opportunity to share with a Jewish college student once. A simple chocolate resulted in a great conversation with him about the Messiah and Old Testament prophecy. He was very interested and hadn't heard any of that before.

4) Use your romance, or lack thereof, to point to Jesus. You could talk up your spouse on Valentine's day, explaining how God has blessed you and describing your relationship with Christ as the glue that holds the relationship together. If you're not married, share how you're trusting God and following Him concerning purity. That's the last thing on most peoples' minds on Valentine's day but it will always bring up conversations about why you believe what you believe.

5) Host an event or dinner for all the single ladies in your sphere of influence. Many of our college guys will put together Valentine's dinners each year just to honor the many women who won't have dates on Valentine's Day. They always make it very

special, with decorations, roses and more. They use the dinner as an opportunity to share Christ with these women who are often acutely aware of their lack of a date.

6) Put evangelistic, Valentine's Day or love related comments or videos on your social media.

Those are just a few ideas for sharing Christ on Valentine's Day. I hope you'll try them out next Valentine's.

Evangelism Idea # 75 - How to share your faith on St. Patrick's Day.

I don't usually celebrate St. Patrick's Day. In fact, I've never done anything for St. Patrick's Day. I don't even wear green and usually forget it completely. That's no excuse not to share the Gospel on St. Patrick's Day! Here are a few ways you can do that.

1) Tell the true story of St. Patrick. St. Patrick helped abolish slavery in Ireland and ended up leading much of that Island to Christ. He was a very successful missionary and a tremendous figure. Definitely check out the history of St. Patrick for more on his evangelism strategy. Use his story to initiate evangelistic conversations.

2) Ask people if they believe in luck. Then, use that topic to transition to a spiritual topic and then a conversation about Jesus!

3) Post a video, question or evangelistic statement on your social media. One great video would be a video titled CTRL Z produced by the Global Short Films Network (get the video at globalshortfilmnetwork.com). You could post that video along with the question, "What would you do if you could be so lucky?" That

will undoubtedly start some interesting conversations.

4) Have a local Christian Celtic band (if you happen to have one in your area) do an evangelistic concert. We have a local band named *Patrick Crossing* which often does this type of thing (thanks CJ!).

Well, I hope you get a chance to try each of these next St. Patrick's Day!

Evangelism Idea # 76 - How to share your faith on Easter.

Easter is one of the greatest times of the year to share your faith! Of course, witnessing should be a lifestyle and there is never a bad time to share the Good News of Jesus. The following Easter evangelism ideas will help you share the greatest news in history on Easter. Some of these came from Cru's *10 Easter evangelism ideas* and Evangelism.net's *6 Easter evangelism ideas*. Each of those posts have other ideas I haven't listed here and I've also added a few others. Try these fourteen ideas next Easter.

1) Invite people to a sunrise service or your church's Easter service.

2) Do an Easter Egg hunt with Resurrection Eggs (just search "resurrection eggs" on Amazon). Invite friends' and relatives' kids over and share the real reason for Easter. This activity will open up conversations with the parents about the Gospel as well.

3) Share the evidence for the resurrection. There are a ton of great reasons to believe, with confidence, that Jesus rose from that grave two thousand years ago. Share that evidence with your

friends. Go to garyhabermas.com for great resources and evidence for the resurrection.

4) Give out a great book. Lee Stroble's *The Case for Easter*[31] would be a great little handout. You can get this book in bulk at christianbook.com for $1.49 each.

5) Give your friends an Easter card with an Evangelistic message.

6) Give out a great DVD. You could give friends *The Case for Christ*, *The Passion of the Christ*, *Son of God*, or something different. You could also just invite them over to watch the movie with you. Include a good card.

7) Create an Easter gift basket for friends, co-workers, kids or neighbors. Include an invite to your church, reading material about easter or a movie (you could include some of the ideas above in this gift basket or just keep it simple).

8) Share a short Easter message online, posting a relevant evangelistic comment or video on your social media.

9) Ask someone if they celebrate Easter. Then, work through the sound barriers to share the Gospel with them.

10) Host a Passover celebration. This is a fun, interesting and unique cultural experience that most of your friends would love to be invited to. A lot of churches are starting to do this so you could invite people to a local Passover celebration if there is one happening in your city. The main point is to bring Christ and the Gospel into every aspect of the meal.

11) Host an Easter celebration. Go all out. Host a huge Easter meal and get-together. Invite friends, neighbors and relatives. Then, make sure to mention the reason for the celebration.

12) Bake a bunch of Easter cookies or rolls and share them, and the Gospel, with friends. Google "Easter Cookies" and "Easter Rolls" for more on those ideas (thanks Angi Pratt, for this idea).

13) Witness at Church! There will be many seekers attending your church on Easter. Look for new people who don't regularly attend and find a time to meet up with them so you can clarify the Gospel. Ask them what they thought about the service and then transition to the Gospel from there.

14) Ask people you see the week after Easter what they did for Easter. This will open up a conversation about Easter that you can then bring back to the Gospel.

Easter provides a unique opportunity to share the hope we have in Christ that no other religion or worldview can match. I hope you apply these ideas next Easter!

Evangelism Idea # 77 - How to share your faith on Mother's Day.

Mother's Day, like all other holidays, is a great time to share your faith. Here are five easy ways you can do this.

1) If your mom raised you to love and follow Jesus, honor her by publicly stating that one of things you admire most about her is how she taught you to follow Jesus. Include the Gospel as you share about your mom.

2) If your mom doesn't know the Lord, a great evangelism idea would be to share the Gospel with your mom on Mother's Day.

3) Invite non-Christian friends to a Mother's Day lunch or dinner. Honor your wife, mom and other moms who are present, especially if they love Jesus. Also, share the stories of good Biblical moms (for example, Jochebed, Mary, Eunice, etc.).

4) Ask women you meet on Mother's Day if they are mothers. If so, tell them, "Happy Mother's Day," and then transition the conversations to the Gospel.

5) Share a God-glorifying, Mother's Day post or video on your social media.

Whatever you do, don't miss the opportunity to share the Good News on Mother's Day.

Evangelism Idea # 78 - How to share your faith on Memorial Day.

Memorial Day is the day we remember those who have died for our country. The parallel to the Gospel is impossible to miss. Here are a two ways you can share the Gospel on Memorial Day.

1) Celebrate Memorial Day with a BBQ and friends. While you discuss the sacrifices some have made so we can be here today, bring up John 15:13 and use that as a transition point to what Jesus did for us.

2) Post John 15:13 on your social media and include a link to a Youtube video with a Gospel message.

Jesus said it best, "Greater love has no one than this, that he lay down his life for his friends" (Jn. 15:13). This is true of His payment for our sins and of the sacrifices so many have made for us.

Evangelism Idea # 79 - How to share your faith on Father's Day.

This Father's Day, get into a great conversation about Christ by asking someone what they love most about Father's day or how they plan to celebrate Father's Day. Next, ask them which characteristics they think epitomize the perfect father. You could begin working through the sound barriers from there, including other questions about fathers. As you transition, bring up the fatherly characteristics of God and help them see their heavenly Father as the only perfect father. If it is appropriate, you could also ask them if they could have changed anything, what would they have changed about their earthly dads. You can tell them that only God can meet those needs and continue sharing from there. Many people negatively attribute the character flaws of their dads to God. Help them see that God is the perfect Father; He is compassionate (Ps. 103:13) and patient (2 Peter 3:9), He protects (Ps. 91:4), provides (Phil. 4:19), forgives (Ps. 103:3), gently disciplines (Pr. 3:11-12, Heb. 12:5-13), helps (Gen. 49:25), comforts (Jn. 14:26), sacrificially serves (Mt. 20:28) and unconditionally loves us (Jer. 31:3, Jn. 3:16).

I hope you have a wonderful Father's Day and I hope you'll get a chance to share the Good News about our Heavenly Father with someone this Father's Day. That will be a great way to celebrate Father's day and there is no better gift that you could ever give your heavenly Father for Father's day!

Evangelism Idea # 80 - How to share your faith on the Fourth of July.

Sometime over the course of the Fourth of July holiday, tell someone, "Happy Fourth of July," or ask them what they're doing for the Fourth of July. Just bring up the Fourth of July. Once you're discussing the Fourth of July, ask them what they think freedom is all about. Listen to their answer. Then, ask them if they feel like they are experiencing true freedom personally. Those are the transition questions and they lead to a very obvious direction setting question. Ask them if they have three minutes for you to briefly tell them how you found freedom in Jesus Christ. Then, share your testimony (keep this short and prepare by writing your testimony first; you can do that in the testimony evangelism idea in chapter ten). Make sure to include the Gospel and Galatians 5:1 (that would be a great verse to post on your social media on the Fourth as well) as you share your testimony and ask them what they think when you are done. This type of conversation would be good in any setting but would be even better if you invite the person you're sharing with over for a Fourth of July BBQ. I hope you get a chance to do this on the Fourth of July!

Evangelism Idea # 81 - How to share your faith on Labor Day.

Why do you do what you do? Before working in full time ministry, I was an Air Quality Specialist. Every week my wonderful co-workers would say over and over again, "another day another dollar." There was no guiding purpose in their careers. Many workers in today's workforce are frustrated with their current jobs and searching for something better. That being said, a lot of people out there are spending the majority of their time, energy and life on something they aren't passionate about. Most people are clueless about why they are here and what they are here for.

Contrast that with the purpose God has created you for (Eph. 2:10, Jer. 29:11) and the abundant life found only in Him (Jn. 10:10). For most of us, the workplace is the biggest area God has called us to reach. Over an average lifetime most of us will spend 75,000 hours at work. That's 75,000 hours of opportunities given to us by God to reach this world for Him (Col. 4:5). Remember He put you where you are, for this very time, to reach your sphere of influence for Him (Acts 17:26-27).

That brings us to the next evangelism idea! This is so simple. Ask someone you meet on Labor Day, or someone at work, why they do what they do. Ask young people you meet what they plan to do with their lives and why. Listen to their answers. No matter what happens it will be a great conversation starter and one that can easily be transitioned back to the Good News. When they ask you why you do what you do, you can tell them about your life purpose! As you discuss your life purpose remember to share the reason for that: Jesus in you (in fact, the two verses before Eph. 2:10, the great verse on purpose listed above, discuss this; check out Eph. 2:8-9)! This is a great starting point for the Gospel so go into your testimony or a presentation of the Gospel from there.

As you share your faith on Labor Day, make sure to keep applying the ideas for reaching your workplace mentioned earlier in this book as well. Remember, your workplace is one of the greatest mission fields you'll ever have the opportunity of reaching. I hope you have a blast taking the initiative to reach people for Christ on Labor Day!

Evangelism Idea # 82 - How to share your faith on September 11ᵗʰ.

September 11ᵗʰ is not a holiday and it is a date we'd all rather forget but, since we're reminded every year of the events that transpired on that date, it is an obvious opportunity for evangelism. Next September 11ᵗʰ, ask someone where they were on September 11ᵗʰ. As the conversation unfolds, transition to a spiritual conversation by discussing Islam, terrorism, the Middle East, the problem of evil or any number of issues (if you're talking about these things with a Muslim, refer to the notes on reaching out to Muslims earlier in the book). Then, transition that spiritual conversation back to the Gospel and share the hope we have in Jesus even in spite of such terror.

Evangelism Idea # 83 - How to share your faith on Halloween.

Halloween is a holiday some Christians avoid like the plague but it doesn't have to be! It can be a great time for sharing the Good News. Here are a few Halloween evangelism ideas.

1) Do a reverse trick-or-treat spiritual interest survey. Everyone else is going door-to-door on Halloween night so why not you? Buy a bunch of candy, then go through your community, going door-to-door. When people open the door say, "surprise, can we give you some candy?" They'll probably laugh and ask what's up. Then, mention that you are involved with a local church or ministry doing a short Halloween survey. Ask them questions that

relate back to the Gospel and make sure to follow up with them if they're interested. Get more information on spiritual interest surveys in chapter ten.

2) Give trick-or-treaters candies with verses and evangelistic messages attached to them.

3) My dad, one of the most diligent evangelists I know, shared this idea with me: put a sign on the outside of your door that says, "ask about the Spirit that lives in this house." Then, share the Gospel and the reality of the Holy Spirit with those who ask.

4) Get involved with a local church's Halloween activities. Many churches do Halloween outreaches and these provide a great opportunity for evangelism.

5) Finally, make sure not to neglect to share the Gospel with your own kids on Halloween. Tell them what the holiday is all about and then clarify the Gospel for them as well.

These ideas are sure to turn this godless holiday around for the better so don't just blow Halloween off this year, make it your best Halloween ever!

Evangelism Idea # 84 - How to share your faith on Veteran's Day.

I always like to thank veterans for their service whenever I see them and I'm sure you do too. You can apply this idea whether you are thanking a veteran or talking with someone about Veteran's Day. Next time you're discussing Veteran's Day, veterans' service or thanking a veteran, tell them, "thank you," for giving the ultimate sacrifice by putting their life on the line for our freedom.

Then, as with the Memorial Day evangelism idea, tell them John 15:13 says, "Greater love has no one than this, that he lay down his life for his friends." Tell them you're thankful to them for doing just that and then ask them if they've ever heard that quote before. If they say no you'll have a good idea they probably don't know Jesus. However they answer, you'll find yourself in the middle of a great conversation about Jesus and an awesome opportunity to share the Good News.

Evangelism Idea # 85 - How to share your faith on Thanksgiving.

Thanksgiving is definitely a favorite in our house. It also provides a unique opportunity to share the Good News with family, friends and anyone you might cross paths with. Below are a few ideas for how to do just that.

1) Send out a few messages to friends and family members that won't be with you on Thanksgiving. You could do this with Facebook, a text message, a phone call or an e-mail. Tell them Happy Thanksgiving and then mention that today you are thankful for all God's blessings in your life, including them. Finish by telling them God loves them dearly. This will be a kind message that will bring up an evangelistic conversation with that loved one.

2) Post what you're thankful for (specifically the salvation you've found in Jesus) on your social media. That will be a witness to each of your online friends.

3) Share a similar message at Thanksgiving dinner with any friends and family that happen to be with you. Before getting started, mention what you are thankful for and mention first and foremost what Jesus did at the Cross so we could each have peace

with God. Keep it short and sweet but don't miss this great opportunity to share.

4) If you'll be out and about, tell people you meet "Happy Thanksgiving," and then ask them what they're thankful for. You could also ask who they're thankful to. That will most likely open up an opportunity for you to share the same with them. Once again, bring it back to Jesus!

5) Host a Thanksgiving party. Invite friends and family members over for a time of eating, fun, reflection and discussion. You'll find it is a great way to share your faith with your loved ones. Make sure to pray for your dinner, pointing to Jesus before you eat.

I hope these ideas work well for you and I hope you get to share the Good News. As you consider these Thanksgiving evangelism ideas, thank God for the privilege of partnering with Him to share the Good News. He sure doesn't need us but it is a real blessing that He invites us to be a part of what He is doing in this world (1 Cor. 3:9).

Evangelism Idea # 86 - How to share your faith on Christmas.

Christmas is probably the easiest time of the year to share the Good News. Even non-Christians are naturally thinking about spiritual things during the holidays (it's impossible not to considering all the spiritually themed decorations and music). It's also a time of year when many are depressed and sad. They need the hope that you have. Here are twenty-five easy and creative ways that you can share your faith this Christmas season! These are just a start and I hope they encourage you. If you're diligent, you can do one each day from December 1st through Christmas Day.

Ask God for wisdom and for more creative ideas and I'm sure He will bring even more Christmas evangelism ideas to your mind (James 1:5).

1) Be creative with how you decorate the inside and outside of your home. Find ornaments and decorations for your interior that will point visitors to Jesus. It's your house so go all out. Have fun for the glory of God! As far as the outside decorating goes, the sky's the limit. You could spell out an evangelistic message in lights, put out a lit nativity set or do something as simple as setting up a cross of lights. Each of these simple decorating ideas will add a little Christmas cheer to viewers' lives and point them back to Jesus, the reason for the season!

2) Send out Christmas cards that will share your faith with your friends. Once you find the right cards, be creative as you consider what to write. Be sensitive but ready to share the Good News of Christmas with the people you love dearly.

3) Share at the post office. Any time you find yourself in a line think of it as an opportunity to share your faith. I won't lie, it isn't always the first thing that comes to my mind either but the Holy Spirit in you will be quick to remind you! It's really pretty simple. Just nod at the person in front of you when you enter and make some comment about the line (just don't complain too much). You could ask something like, "how long have you been here?" Since it's Christmas ask a Christmas related question like, "sending out last minute Christmas gifts?" Then, ask an easy follow up question about whether or why they celebrate Christmas. Then begin working through the sound barriers. Those will be easy with this topic. If the line is long enough, and it probably will be, you may just get to go through the whole Gospel with someone while you wait. There may even be eavesdroppers who will hear the Gospel. I was doing this once and after the person I was witnessing to left, the person who had been behind me, who had previously heard me teach on evangelism at a local church, said, "way to go, I

was praying for you the whole time."

4) If you're going to be spending time shopping before Christmas, make it a point to share your faith while you're out. You could easily share with someone you find yourself in line next to. You could also share with any of the store employees or cashiers that help you out. Have a simple conversation starting question ready, like, "How is Christmas going for you?" Then work through the sound barriers and share the Good News with them. Just be sensitive about their schedule, they are on the clock and very busy. So whether you share with a store employee or just another shopper, make sure to share the Good News while out buying gifts this Christmas season.

5) Give an evangelistic gift. Picking the right gift can always be difficult but it shouldn't be hard to pick a good, evangelistic gift for your loved ones. Make sure to include a good evangelistic card as well. You could buy your loved one a Bible. Even if they aren't a believer, you can buy them a high quality gift Bible that would look nice on their bookshelf and would be there the next time they became interested in investigating further. You could get them a good Christian book or DVD. You could buy them a classic movie that points to Jesus! *A Charlie Brown Christmas*, *It's a Wonderful Life* or *The Nativity Story* would all work well. You could also make them a creative gift bag. Whatever gifts you end up buying, don't miss the opportunity to point those you love most back to Jesus.

6) Serve people this Christmas. Good works are never a substitute for evangelism but they can be a great transition to the Gospel. Christmas can be a great time to serve others and use that as a way to share the Good News. Apply some of the servant evangelism ideas listed previously next Christmas season.

7) Help someone this Christmas. Times are tough! Many are out of work and many more are under-employed. I'm sure there are numerous people in your sphere of influence that are pretty needy this holiday season. A great way to share your faith

with them could be to start by sharing some money or food or helping them with whatever need they may have. They may even just need some presents for their kids. Every one of them is at a place where they are probably very open to the Gospel and will be even more when believers share both physically and spiritually with them.

8) Tell people about Santa. Santa is real! You probably already knew that. I'm obviously not talking about the pudgy character dressed in red! Our society has lost the true meaning of Christmas and perverted it with a commercial perspective epitomized by the character we call Santa Claus. Erin and I have never led our kids to believe in Santa (or any other fictional characters) but have found the topic is a great way to transition back to Jesus and the Gospel. Next time you hear people talking about Santa, go ahead and tell them the real story. Nicholas was a wealthy man, orphaned as a boy, who loved God and desired to serve Him. Because Scripture tells us to give to the poor, he spent his life, as a minister, giving away his wealth and providing for the needs of children and the needy. Many of the traditions we have about Santa Claus arose from his efforts. Tell people the true story of a man who loved God so much that he was willing to give all he had to love others as well. That will give you an interesting and easy start to sharing about the greatest gift ever given, the gift that inspired Nicholas to give the way he did and the gift that we celebrate at Christmas, Jesus!

9) Share with your co-workers this Christmas. Decorating your office with a few Christ centered Christmas cards, pictures or posters is a good start. Even if you don't have an office, you could come up with creative ideas to bring Christ into your surroundings. Maybe it could be the Christmas music you play or some other idea. A visible reference to Jesus in your office is a great way to share your faith in your workplace this Christmas. A second way would be to carefully select Christmas cards that share the Gospel for each of your co-workers. A third idea would be to pick Christ centered gifts for your Christmas party. You could also help a co-

worker out, creating an opportunity to share the Gospel. Finally, say Merry Christmas instead of Happy Holidays. That could easily open up discussions with co-workers.

10) Next time you're in town ask your cashier or clerk wherever you happen to be doing errands, or your server at a restaurant, if they celebrate Christmas. If they say, "no," ask what they celebrate. Last time someone told me, "no", I asked what they celebrate and the lady said, "Nothing, I was raised a Jehovah's Witness." I asked if she was still practicing and she said, "no." I asked what she thought about spiritual issues and she said something to the effect of, "searching and open." That opened up a conversation about Christ and a continuing opportunity to share. If they say they do celebrate Christmas, ask them what they celebrate about Christmas. That might catch them off guard but no matter what it will open up into a natural conversation about the meaning of Christmas, Jesus!

11) Tell someone what you want for Christmas (thanks Angi Pratt for this great idea). We always get asked what it is that we want for Christmas. Simply state that that's a hard question to answer because you already have more than you could ever ask for, the greatest gift of all, a relationship with Jesus. You can easily tie this back to Christmas and share the Gospel. Another simple way to transition to the Gospel from a conversation each of us are bound to have numerous times this year!

12) Share *A Charlie Brown Christmas*. A Charlie Brown Christmas has a clear reading of Luke 2:8-14 and a clear description of the real meaning of Christmas, a Savior born to all people. You can often watch it for free on Hulu and Netflix (spread the word this Christmas season). The next time you're talking about Christmas bring up *A Charlie Brown Christmas* and then tie it back to the Gospel or just invite a friend to watch it with you and then talk about it afterwards.

13) Do a Christmas Soularium survey. You'll read about the Soularium tool in chapter ten. Simply alter it a bit, asking three different questions. You could ask, "Which picture or pictures describe what you look forward to most over the holidays?" Then ask, "Which picture or pictures describe how you will celebrate the holidays?" And finally, ask, "Which picture describes what you think is the meaning of Christmas?" These questions will lead to an incredible conversation about Christmas and the meaning of Christmas, Jesus!

14) Give out Christmas gift bags. This is another great idea from Trisha Ramos of *Fish with Trish* (fishwithtrish.com). Make a few gift bags that you could give out to friends, co-workers and neighbors before everyone heads their own ways for Christmas. Include a few small treats along with a short evangelistic message.

15) Share the Gospel while having fun! Whether you'll be traveling or sticking around town having fun, take the initiative to share the Gospel during your free time this Christmas. If you're just out on the town, try sharing with any waiters, waitresses or baristas you meet. If your hitting up the slopes, take advantage of all those lift rides with strangers. I can't even count all the great evangelistic conversations I've had riding the lifts with strangers. Whatever you happen to be doing, remember that vacation time should be a vacation from work, not from sharing the Good News. Witnessing is one of the greatest joys in life and making it a part of your free time this Christmas is sure to make your Christmas even better. Whatever fun activities you have planned this Christmas, make Jesus and telling others about Him, part of those plans!

16) Share the Good News while traveling! Many of us travel during the holidays. If you will be traveling, make it a point to share the Good News with those you encounter along the way. You may never see them again and this may be the only opportunity you ever get to share with them. If you're flying you'll have numerous opportunities to share with people in airports and planes. You could easily start a conversation by asking them where

they're traveling to and then working through the sound barriers from there. If you're driving you could tell a cashier at the gas station "Merry Christmas" and that Jesus loves them. Who knows what will happen when you take the initiative to share as you travel over the holidays!

17) Invite a friend to a Christmas production somewhere in your area. You could invite someone to a Christmas Eve service, a live nativity or a Christmas themed movie. Events like these are fun and Christmasy ways to bring up Christ with your friends. Everyone likes being invited to events like these and whether they come or not, as soon as you invite them you've initiated a conversation that can be brought back to the Gospel easily.

18) Share the Good News with kids. It might not seem like evangelism but it is. Our kids need to hear the Good News as much as any stranger on the street. They are being bombarded with false descriptions of the meaning of Christmas and it is more important than ever that they need to hear the real meaning of Christmas. You wouldn't believe how many college students we meet each year that grew up in Christian families but have never heard the Gospel. You could intentionally share the Gospel using some of the ideas I've already shared or by doing a Christmas Advent together. Most importantly, just make it a point to go over the Christmas story from the Gospels with them. Make sure to discuss the significance of Christ's birth and why He had to come, live, die and be risen to pay the price for our sins so each of us could have peace with God. What a great celebration. So whether they're your kids, grandkids, nieces, nephews or just youngsters that happen to be celebrating with you, make sure to share the Gospel with them this Christmas!

19) Wear a pin. My friend Mark Hohle challenged us all to apply this idea at a recent men's retreat. It is pretty simple. Wear a pin that reminds people why we celebrate Christmas. Make sure it is visible and be ready to get into conversations when people see it. This might not be everybody's favorite idea but it is one more way

to share your faith over Christmas.

20) Get online. You could post an evangelistically themed Christmas message or video on your social media, send an e-mail with a nice Christmas note or message or you could send a Christmas e-card. Whatever you do, bring Christ into your internet world this Christmas!

21) Go caroling. My friend Gerry Geraghty does this every year. The carols we sing at Christmas time are full of the Good News and peoples' hearts are open to Christ's message in a special way this time of year. Christmas caroling can be a great way to share the Good News during Christmas time! Here are eleven great carols with evangelistic messages. *Silent Night, The First Noel, Oh Come, All Ye Faithful, Hark the Herald Angels Sing, Angels We Have Heard on High, Joy to the World, From Heaven Above to Earth I come, Do you hear what I hear, Away in a Manger, God Rest Ye Merry Gentlemen* and *O Holy Night* are all Christmas carols that include evangelistic lyrics. After caroling, make sure to try to share the Gospel with your listeners and even any non-Christians who go caroling with you.

22) Throw a Christmas party. Throw a Christmas party before Christmas and invite a ton of friends (especially those you want to share the Good News with). Plan the event in such a way that you can clearly refer to the Gospel and share with your loved ones in a very warm and friendly way.

23) Talk about candy canes. I'm sure you'll have lots of guests over for Christmas or be a guest along with many others at someone else's place. Candy canes are a great intro to share the Gospel, especially with children. Tradition tells us that the candy cane's "J" shape should remind us of Jesus and when flipped around, it reminds us of a shepherd's staff and how each of us are His sheep. The white color of the candy cane stands for purity. The large red stripe reminds us of His blood which He shed for our sins to make us pure before God. The three small stripes represent the trinity. Talk about a great way to get to the Gospel

from something that will most likely be a decoration wherever you spend Christmas. You could also give out candy canes with a short message including this information attached.

24) Share during your Christmas celebrations. When family and friends are gathered next Christmas, make sure to share the Gospel with them in a sensitive way. Before they arrive, pray for each of your non-Christian relatives. Don't forget the "divine order," talk to God about people (in this case, your loved ones) and then talk to your loved ones about God. Once you're together with them, use some of the following ideas to get into conversations. There are numerous ways to share Christ during your celebrations. Whether you're the host or just attending, you could spice up the Christmas party by taking everyone to a Christmas Eve service, singing some great evangelistic Christmas carols together, watching a good movie or telling people about the significance of candy canes or the true story of Santa. Make sure to read the Christmas story from the Gospels and relate it to the reason Christ had to come in the first place. Don't forget to share with the kids you're celebrating with as well, they need Jesus too! Another opportunity to share is praying before the meal, which is a great way to point your loved ones back to Jesus. Whatever you do, just be willing and take the initiative and look for the opportunities God will bring up!

25) This last Christmas evangelism idea sounds a little goofy but it's worth a try. My friend Gerry Geraghty also came up with this one. He asks, "would there be a Christmas if there were no Easter?" That's a great question and one that has led to the Gospel every time I've asked it. Sometime throughout the course of the day try telling someone, "Happy Easter," and then just wait for a response. If they don't say anything you can just tell them you're asking that question to see how people respond and then ask whether they think there would be a Christmas if there weren't also an Easter. If they do catch you, ask the same question. In both cases, be ready to share the Good News.

Once Christmas is over, continue asking friends and relatives how their celebrations went, transitioning those conversations to the Gospel as well. Christmas is a special time of year. What better way to celebrate than by sharing the meaning of Christmas with people?

Go for it!

Don't get caught up in the selfishness that characterizes so many of our holidays. These are incredible opportunities for evangelism. Decide to make the most of them and I'm confident you'll experience more holiday cheer than ever before! Remember, you don't have what it takes but the Holy Spirit in you does. Take the initiative, in the power of the Holy Spirit and then trust God to come through in the lives of those you share with!

Chapter **10**

Fifteen Ministry Evangelism Ideas

"Jesus' teaching made some people furious. Just make sure it's your ideas that offend and not you, that your beliefs cause the dispute and not your behavior."[32] - Gregory Koukl

Some people are terrified of "ministry evangelism" because they are convinced that offending someone might kill them. That is not the case. Jesus called us to "go and make disciples of all nations" (Matt. 28:19). That requires taking the initiative to go to people with His Good News. Do that as lovingly as possible, understanding that if they still get offended, that is not your problem. Paul's charge to Timothy, concerning this type of evangelism, is a pertinent one for us today, "do the work of an evangelist, discharge all the duties of your ministry" (2 Tim. 4:5). This chapter will focus on ministry mode evangelism ideas. Since this is the type of evangelism that often scares people spit-less, and since a few good ideas can eliminate the majority of that fear, this chapter will be an invaluable resource. These ideas will all focus on evangelism tools that are extremely helpful in ministry. Some say that these evangelistic tools no longer work; that's nonsense and likely indicative of their neglect of evangelism. The Gospel is the power of God (Rom. 1:16) regardless of what format you present it in. Good tools are helpful in sharing your faith. Here are fifteen of them that are guaranteed to work.

Evangelism Idea # 87 - Use a transferable conversational tool to share the Gospel.

These tools include a simple but complete summary of the Gospel and they are great conversation starters. My preferred evangelistic conversational tool is Cru's *Knowing God Personally* booklet. You can ask, "Have you ever seen the Name of the tool you are using, for example, the *Knowing God Personally* booklet?" You can show a person how to receive Christ in a short period of time. They begin with a positive, "God loves you." They clearly present how to receive Christ. They build confidence (you know what you're going to say before you say it). And most importantly, it is a transferable method for teaching others to witness. Anyone can use it. In fact, Master Plan Ministries president Russ Akins once shared the Four Spiritual Laws with a guy who was adamant about not being interested. Russ told him to take the tract and throw it in a junk drawer in case he wanted to look at it later. A while later, the guy returned. He told Russ, "You know that booklet you gave me? It wasn't for me but I gave it to my roommate and it was for him. He prayed the prayer at the end and everything." Russ was then able to contact the guy and follow up with him. The point is, this is a good tool anyone can use.

When you use evangelistic tools, make them less "canned" and avoid a "canned approach" by reading, then illustrating and finally personalizing what you share. When using the KGP or similar evangelistic presentations, remember the following guidelines. Expose the Gospel, don't impose on the person. Go in love, in the power and direction of the Holy Spirit; make sure Christ is on the throne. Pray, remembering the "Divine Order." You are called to present the Gospel clearly in the power of the Holy Spirit. Trust God with the results. Always present the opportunity for a response but don't force it. Without an adequate understanding of the Gospel there can't be a legitimate response.

Again, the idea that these tools no longer work is crazy! A young lady that recently put her faith in Christ in our ministry, after hearing a Four Spiritual Laws presentation, posted this on Facebook: "Little yellow books scare me. But I wonder if the little yellow book had a point to it. If it did, why haven't I [followed Jesus] sooner? Frankly, the thought is terrifying. I wonder what family and friends would say. But I'm still in the midst of a decision. I need support, and I am frightened to tell so many of my friends what I am thinking about Jesus and God. I fear their ridicule. I know they can be cruel. But I'm searching my already tortured soul for an answer. I don't want to be hurt anymore." She put her trust in Christ shortly after making these comments.

You can get the print versions of these tools or get the God Tools app for your phone. I know using a good Gospel conversational tool will help you accurately communicate the whole Gospel each time you share while doing it in a way that anyone who happens to be with you could do as well. That's why we call them transferable tools, you can easily teach and equip young believers to share their faith using them. You can never have too many tools! See an example of how to use this tool at youtube.com/watch?v=fSmeNVvKRZ4. After watching the training video, role play using the KGP with a Christian friend. Don't believe the lie that God can't use a good tool like this. I've personally seen more people than I can remember trust Christ using these tools.

Evangelism Idea # 88 - Use your testimony to share the Gospel.

Personal testimonies drive our economy. Case in point: want to dominate all you do and be the world's best like Tiger Woods, Roger Federer and Thierry Henry? Just shave with a Gillette razor. Of course! Who didn't know those athletes dominated their sports because of their choices in morning hygiene? Testimonies drive our economy because they work. Your personal testimony is a powerful tool. It has been said that "a man with a testimony will never be at the mercy of a man with an argument." No one can deny what God has done in your life.

Go ahead and carefully put together your personal testimony, the story of what God has done in your life, using the testimony worksheet in appendix D. Putting it on paper and memorizing it will equip you to be ready to share it at any moment. This will take a little bit of time but once you've done it you'll remember it for years to come. You will "always be prepared to give an answer to everyone who asks you to give the reason for the hope that you have" (1 Peter 3:15). Your testimony is a powerful tool.

You could also do a recovery testimony. In addition to your salvation testimony, write out a similar short testimony of how God has rescued you from some type of sin. You could explain how His power has given you victory over addictions, lust, pride, or any number of personal vices. Use this recovery testimony with both believers and non-believers, allowing them to see the power of Christ in your life as a believer.

Remember the Samaritan woman and the many people who believed because of her testimony (John 4). Also, remember the promise of Revelation 12:11! So, don't waste any more time, work through the testimony worksheet in appendix D now. Do your best to carefully articulate who you were before Christ, the Gospel, how you trusted Christ and what He has done since. He is the focus and this tool is just another way to share the Good News with people that desperately need Jesus. If you want a great Biblical example of a "three minute testimony" check out Paul's strategic use of this tool, in court, in Acts 26 (time how long it takes you to read that passage just for fun). Finally, look for an opportunity soon to share your testimony!

Evangelism Idea # 89 - Use a short Spiritual interest survey to share the Gospel.

This idea is simple but sweet, tested and true, an oldie but a goodie! It is great because it instantly destroys the first two of the four sound barriers. This tool is the short spiritual interest survey. We typically meet hundreds of people every time we do our spiritual interest survey push and we always have numerous evangelistic conversations and salvations that result. You'll also meet Christians you can follow up with doing this.

It is critical that you develop a simple and short survey. Our surveys usually ask five simple questions: 1) What is your name? 2) What is your spiritual or church background? 3) On a scale of one to ten, with ten being positive, what do you think about Jesus? 4) On a scale of one to ten, with ten being positive, how important is it to you to pursue spiritual things? And 5) We are passionate about sharing Jesus' message of love, forgiveness and life with people we meet. Which of the following options sounds best to you: A) talking more about Jesus with someone over coffee, B) getting invites to different events our ministry puts on, C) all of the above or D) none of the above? If they want to be contacted we then get their info for follow up. These surveys always work! Get more survey ideas at crupressgreen.com/surveys-and-questionnaires.

Once you develop a short survey, pray and then go in the power of the Holy Spirit. Walk up to somebody and ask, "We're a part of a local church (or ministry) here in town and we're trying to get to know what people in the community think about spiritual issues; do you have a few minutes for a short spiritual interest survey?" Go through the short survey, it should only take a minute or two. Be ready to share the Good News if the opportunity comes up during the survey but don't worry if it doesn't. If they don't want to go that direction, that's fine, just finish the survey and ask if they'd like to get together in the future to talk more about Jesus. If they say, "yes," take the initiative to follow up with them shortly. If they say, "no," don't worry about it, just trust God with them. Either way, make sure to have a few tracts or other information you could give them before they leave. Remember, take the initiative in the power of the Holy Spirit and trust the results to God. Go have some fun with this simple tool!

Surveys are powerful tools. I once surveyed a freshman college student who listed a spiritual interest of six out of ten. About a week later, he asked if he could do it again. I thought that was strange but said he could. He then listed a ten out of ten. I asked him what had changed. He told me how he had clinically died the past week of alcohol poisoning (yes, this is the second instance of that sort of amazing story in this book! Praise God for preserving these young peoples' lives). The medics managed to revive him but his brush with death left him spiritually searching. He put his trust in Christ that day. This conversation never would have happened if it wasn't for that survey!

I doubt you'll find an easier way to initiate a spiritual conversation. Surveys have worked for years and they're no less effective today. Decide to use this great tool, it will result in countless evangelistic conversations and decisions for Christ.

Evangelism Idea # 90 - Use the Soularium to share the Gospel.

The *Soularium* tool is one of the greatest tools I've ever found. You can use this tool conversationally by just walking up to strangers and asking, "Have you ever seen the Soularium before?" They'll usually say, "no, what is it?" You can tell them it is a picture survey about life's biggest questions. I always mention that it is a creative way for the listener to share their views with us. You can also use it at a table or a desk in a public place (like on a college campus), laying the cards out where passersby will stop, look and ask what they're for.

This tool completely disarms people and destroys walls. I've had people tell me, within minutes of meeting them, "I want to be pure again but I don't know how," "I am searching," "I feel like everything around me is dark and I know the light is out there, I am looking but haven't found it yet," "I want my soul to go up (to heaven)," "I feel like I am rusted out, falling apart, broken and I need someone to come and help me" and other similar comments. If you think it would be great having people open up like that within moments of meeting them, you need to get your hands on this tool and use it often. This tool works anywhere and everywhere. You can get the tool at campuscrusade.com/catalog/SOULARIUM.html.

Last summer, Master Plan staff guys Brad Jones and Malcolm Hillewaert were using this tool on Main Street, right here in Durango, Colorado. They met a middle-aged man who told them he had been praying every day for a month that someone would share Christ with him. They shared with him and He put his trust in Christ. The Soularium is a great tool that makes stories like that one possible.

Evangelism Idea # 91 - Use a t-shirt to share the Gospel.

This idea is awesome because you will probably not have to do a whole lot to start a conversation (although I hope you won't quit trying). This is super simple. The idea is to wear a great conversation starting Christian t-shirt. Don't pick anything silly but try to pick one that will pique peoples' curiosity. I suggest buying one from liveoffensively.com if you need one (their whole purpose is to create t-shirts that will bring up evangelistic conversations every time you wear them). We met these guys and they are big time evangelists! The point is to wear a great Christian shirt that will get you into spiritual conversations. If you have a typical office job and if your office does "Casual Fridays," this is a great time to be intentional about doing something easy that will have tremendous fruit (I used to do this at my pre-ministry office job and it was a blast). So get a good t-shirt, wear it and be ready to share the Gospel when people ask what the shirt is all about. Make sure to have a tool like the KGP ready if you need one.

Evangelism Idea # 92 - Use the Perspective cards to share the Gospel.

Yet another great tool from CRU Press! The perspective cards ask 1) what is the nature of God, 2) what is human nature, 3) what is life's purpose, 4) who is Jesus and 5) what is the source of truth. For each of those questions there are a number of cards, each with a perspective common today. After the person you are talking with shares their perspective you have the opportunity to share the Biblical perspective on each of those topics. It ends up being a great way to get into deep spiritual conversations and share the Good News in a relatively short period of time. Get the Perspective cards at crupress.com/products/perspective-cards.

Evangelism Idea # 93 - Use Jesus' own words to share the Gospel.

Many people today have fairly low opinions of the church (they think church is religion and religion is bad), Christians (they think we're all hypocrites) and the Bible (most of them, even Christians, believe it is full of errors). Even though those three opinions are all wrong, we can get into trouble when we package the Gospel as "how the Bible says you can become a Christian." For many, that comes across like, "how this lame book you don't trust tells you how you can become one of those people you despise." Jesus, on the other hand, has a great reputation. Young people across the board think He's great (they may not know who He really is but they think highly of Him). In fact, our surveys consistently report extremely high "favorability ratings" for Jesus. To add to the confusion most people encounter with the Gospel today, most tracts encourage a "personal relationship with Jesus" but rarely if ever even quote Him. Christians know the Bible is all His Word but the non-believer you're talking with hasn't quite gotten there yet. There is a great way to get past these barriers.

This idea uses peoples' high perspective of Jesus to initiate conversations about the Gospel from a better starting point, one of His direct words. Instead of saying, "Do you want to know how the Bible says you can become a Christian" (or something to that effect), you can ask them, "would you like to hear what Jesus says to you personally?" Based on that premise, I put the "Gospel in Jesus' words" up on a blog a while back and it quickly became the most read post on that blog. I have also put it into simple one page handouts and Gospel tract versions. You can copy the text below and use it any way you need.

After initiating a Gospel conversation with someone, simply ask them if you can share Jesus' own words with them. If they say yes, share this Gospel message:

1) Jesus loves you and desires a personal relationship with you! Jesus says, "God so loved the world that he gave His only Son, so that everyone who believes in Him will not perish but have eternal life. Come to me, all of you who are weary and carry heavy burdens, and I will give you rest. I am the light of the world. If you follow me, you won't be stumbling through the darkness, because you will have the light that leads to life. All who put their trust in me will no longer remain in the darkness. My purpose is to give life in all its fullness." (Jn. 3:16 NLT, Matt. 11:28 NLT, Jn. 8:12 NLT, Jn. 12:46 NLT, Jn. 10:10 NLT).

2) Unfortunately, your sin keeps you from that relationship and the purpose God has for you. Jesus says, "Sin is unbelief in me. For out of the heart come evil thoughts, murder, adultery, sexual immorality, theft, false testimony, slander. These are what make a man 'unclean.' Everyone who sins is a slave of sin; they will go away to eternal punishment, but the righteous to eternal life. If you do not believe that I am the one I claim to be, you will indeed die in your sins." (Jn. 16:9 NLT, Matt. 15:19-20 NIV, Jn. 8:34 NLT, Matt. 25:46 NIV, Jn. 8:24 NIV).

3) Jesus is your only hope. Jesus says, "Greater love has no one than this, that he lay down his life for his friends. Everyone who looks to the Son and believes in Him shall have eternal life, and I will raise him up at the last day. They will never be condemned for their sins, but they have already passed from death into life." (Jn. 15:13 NIV, Jn. 6:40 NIV, Jn. 5:24 NLT).

4) You must choose whether you'll receive Jesus as Savior and Lord. Jesus says, "Turn from your sins and believe this Good

News! I am the way, the truth, and the life. No one can come to the Father except through me. No one can see the kingdom of God unless he is born again. I stand at the door and knock. If you hear me calling and open the door, I will come in, and we will share a meal as friends." (Mk. 1:15 NLT, Jn. 14:6 NLT, Jn. 3:3 NIV, Rev. 3:20 NLT).

5) Do you hear Jesus knocking? Do you want to open the door? The Bible tells you exactly how. It says, "if you confess with your mouth, 'Jesus is Lord,' and believe in your heart that God raised him from the dead, you will be saved" (Rom. 10:9) and "it is by grace you have been saved, through faith - and this not from yourselves, it is the gift of God - not by works, so that no one can boast" (Eph. 2:8-9). Do you recognize your sin has separated you from God? Do you want to open the door to your life and allow Jesus to come in and take control? Are you ready to surrender your life to Him, recognizing Him as Lord (please read Lk. 9:23-25)? This is a simple yet life altering decision.

6) You can receive Christ and His forgiveness for your sins right now by putting your faith and trust in Him and inviting Him to take control of your life through prayer. This prayer is not a magic trick that gets you into heaven but rather a personal response to Jesus' call; it is your decision to receive Him, by faith, as your Savior and Lord. You can pray a prayer like this: "Jesus, I realize you want a personal relationship with me. I know I am a sinner and that my sins and selfishness keep me from you. Thank you for dying on the cross for my sins and rising again to give me new life. I surrender myself to you. Please forgive me, come into my life, give me a new life and be my Savior and Lord. Thank you."

Use this as a conversational tool, just like the KGP. You could transition to this tool as you'd transition through the sound barriers to other tools and then just share this and see how it goes. The first time we used this was at an event where I was leading an evangelism team. Fearless evangelist Tim Clemens was trying the tool out and one of the first guys he shared it with put his trust in

Christ and was baptized. Jesus' words are powerful so use them!

Evangelism Idea # 94 - Use the BEST FACTS apologetics tool to share the Gospel.

Most Christians are terrified of apologetics and fear being confronted by an atheist friend. For that reason, I developed the BEST FACTS tool. This tool gives anyone who uses it a short description of why religions and worldviews other than Christianity are false, why the evidence proves God exists and why the Bible is trustworthy. It concludes with an evangelistic presentation. It is also organized into an acronym consisting of four words which you can memorize so you'll "always be prepared to give an answer to everyone who asks you to give the reason for the hope that you have" (1 Peter 3:15). You can get this tool for free at thebestfacts.com. I encourage you to use this tool as a secondary evangelistic tool. If someone is interested in the Gospel and has no objections, don't needlessly bring up apologetics. This tool is designed for those who need a little more evidence before taking the next step. It is also a great resource for anyone who struggles with doubt. Get the BEST FACTS tool today and start using it.

Evangelism Idea # 95 - Use tracts to share the Gospel.

Growing up, I was always amazed how there was a constant stream of these tracts flowing from my dad's hands. He left them everywhere. He would sneak them into books in bookstores, leave them at pay-phones and give them to nearly everyone we met. I've always admired his evangelistic fervor. Some people would say these don't work any longer. They may not be as effective as they once were but it is crazy to write them off. I have a pastor friend who came to Christ by grabbing a tract off the top of a trash can. I have another ministry friend who came to Christ after coming across a tract while trying to commit suicide. Make it a point to get some good, unique, trendy tracts that you can distribute in creative ways. Don't be awkward about it but don't miss this great opportunity either. You can get tracts at gospeltractstore.com, store.livingwaters.com and other sites. Have a blast sharing the Gospel with tracts.

Evangelism Idea # 96 - Use short movies to share the Gospel.

This is a neat new tool and I have had numerous great conversations using it. The basic idea is that you can download and play short, thought-provoking videos on a computer or other type of device. The videos bring up numerous topics that can be related back to the Gospel. It is a great tool for ministry evangelism. You can get the videos and training from the Global Short Film Network at globalshortfilmnetwork.com. Try this idea soon, it is one more tool you should have in your evangelism tool belt.

Evangelism Idea # 97 - Use the eCube to share the Gospel.

The eCube or Evangecube is an e3 tool that works great when sharing the Gospel with children. It seems a bit cheesy for adults (but I'll be the last one to write any evangelism tool off). I've used it with children and even led the first kid I ever shared it with to Christ. The eCube is a folding cube that folds in and out revealing a different part of the Gospel with each move. It is creative, interesting and it effectively communicates the Gospel. It is also a great tool for communicating the Gospel in a very simple and easy to understand way. You can get the eCube at shop.e3resources.org/ecube-classic and make sure to use this when witnessing to children.

Evangelism Idea # 98 - Use the Livingwaters optical illusion cards to share the Gospel.

The optical illusion cards are a great Livingwaters tool that can be a lot of fun. You simply ask someone if they like optical illusions. If they say yes, or ask what you're talking about, just hold up the optical illusion cards and ask them which is bigger. It's an illusion and neither is bigger but it draws the listener into a Gospel presentation. The first card takes the conversation from the illusion and how it affects a persons eyes to a spiritual conversation. The second clarifies the Gospel. Together the cards help you initiate interesting spiritual conversations and share the Gospel. You can get the optical illusion cards at store.livingwaters.com.

Evangelism Idea # 99 - Use the life as we know it tool to share the Gospel.

The life as we know it tool is a unique tool designed to start a conversation with friends, neighbors, family members, co-workers or anyone else you know. You buy the box from lifeasweknow.it. Then you host a get-together, invite people to come, meet up for dinner and then work through the interactive tool, sharing an evening of conversation about life's most important issues. It begins by asking what the beginning of everyone's story was, allowing friends to share about their pasts. Then it asks what their obstacles have been, what their hope is and what they think their future holds. This is just a tool that initiates spiritual conversations and it is a great way to get those conversations rolling. Make sure to be ready with your testimony before hosting one of these events. Also, make sure to clarify the Gospel when you share. Once you've done that, you can continue following up with those you shared with. This is a great tool for witnessing to neighbors and family members. Again, get it at lifeasweknow.it.

Evangelism Idea # 100 - Use your own tools to share the Gospel.

This is not a joke. God has given you His Holy Spirit (Eph. 1:13, 1 Cor. 3:16, 6:19) and His very mind (1 Cor. 2:16). He also promises to give you wisdom when you ask for it (James 1:5). Many of the ideas in this book are ideas that God gave me and various friends of mine and there are even more that wouldn't fit in this book. The *Soularium* tool, one of the greatest I have ever seen, is an idea that came to the Cru team in France as they sought God for wisdom about reaching their spiritually lethargic community for Christ. He answered their prayer and many of us have benefited as a result. I want to challenge you to ask God to give you fresh, new evangelism ideas and then brainstorm with the mind He gave you, in the power of the Holy Spirit in you, coming up with new ideas that will help reach this world for Jesus! God may just give you the next *Soularium* idea. Please get familiar with the tools others have put together. You should visit spreadtruth.com/resources, e3resources.org, evangelismexplosion.org/resources, crupressgreen.com, store.livingwaters.com, and other sites. There are countless other tools all over the place (find even more in appendix E). Familiarize yourself with them. Don't, however, trust those tools more than the Holy Spirit. Use those tools and rely on God's wisdom for tools and ideas that will help you effectively reach your community for Christ.

Evangelism Idea # 101 - Use a top ten prayer list when sharing the Gospel.

This last idea is simple but very important! So important, in fact, that I saved it till the end so it would be on your mind as the book comes to a close. It has been called the "Divine Order" and it goes like this, "first talk to God about people and then talk to people about God." Sounds simple but it is not applied often enough. Prayer is critical in evangelism. It is vitally important to be praying for those you share the Gospel with. It is also critical to invite others to pray for and with you as you minister. Our dear friend Barbara Dunlap is my favorite example of this; on a weekly basis, she asks people to pray God will use her in ministry. Never underestimate the need for or power of prayer.

This last idea is to come up with a top ten list. Sit down and brainstorm through your sphere of influence. Then, write out the names of at least ten people you want to see saved. Begin praying for them every day. The more you pray for them, the more likely you will be to share with them too. One lady has been on my list since February 2008. She recently trusted Christ! I put another guy that I shared with on the list after he cussed over and over about Christians. He also came to Christ and after two years of discipleship, he wants to become a pastor. Another guy I put on the list had been called the worst guy in his dorm. You guessed it, he also trusted Christ. I have to share this last example. Remember the young man I said trusted Christ after being resuscitated after clinically dying of alcohol poisoning? Well the reason that happened was a friend of his who challenged him to finish off a bottle of whisky. I also got to share the Good News with him later on. After praying for him for nearly a whole year and after tons of follow up, he told me that he put his trust in Christ the last day that I saw him on campus. One of the great joys of having a list like this is seeing those prayers answered and being able to take them off the list or move them to a new section!

In case you were wondering about this whole list thing, lists are not unspiritual. Paul wrote in Philemon 1:4, "I always thank my God as I remember you in my prayers." A list is just a memory aide for prayer. Don't make it more important than it is and obviously be flexible to pray as the Holy Spirit directs but do have a memory aide so you won't forget to be praying for those God has put in your sphere of influence!

Here are ten consequences of failing to pray. First, people who fail to pray miss out on the joy of co-laboring with God (1 Cor. 3:9). Instead of the exhilaration of answered prayer, they experience the monotony of ministry routine. Second, people who fail to pray miss out on what God could have done in and through them (James 4:2). God can sovereignly choose not to do what His followers selfishly choose not to pray for. Third, people who fail to pray miss out on God's unparalleled power (Eph. 3:20-21). Evangelism quickly becomes an exercise of the flesh rather than a powerful work produced by faith (1 Thes. 1:3, James 5:16). Fourth, people who fail to pray miss out on God's peace (Phil. 4:6-7). Instead of casting their anxieties on Him (1 Peter 5:7), they struggle to do evangelism on their own, resulting in frustration, burnout and pride. Fifth, people who fail to pray miss out on victory in spiritual battle (Eph. 6:10-20). Instead of wrestling in prayer (Col. 4:12) they resort to passivity and lethargy. Sixth, people who fail to pray miss out on God's blessing (2 Chr. 7:14). Content with the status quo, they arrogantly get stuck with it. Seventh, people who fail to pray miss out on God's heart. Praying in line with God's will (Matt. 6:10, Jn. 14:13-14), unites a believer with His heart for His world,

His people and His ministry; people who fail to pray fail to acquire His heart for those they serve. Eighth, people who fail to pray miss out on God's vision and direction. Instead of prayerfully acquiring God's wisdom (James 1:5), they negligently rely on their own. Ninth, people who fail to pray miss out on partnership with other believers. Prayer is an instrumental component of authentic fellowship (Acts 2:42) and people who fail to pray for other believers alienate themselves from them. Finally, people who fail to pray miss out on intimacy with God. Instead of uninterrupted intimacy with their Savior (Jn. 15:5, 1 Thes. 5:17), they experience only a fraction of the fellowship they could be having with Him. This is undoubtedly the worst consequence of failing to pray.

Remember Samuel's words, "far be it from me that I should sin against the LORD by failing to pray for you" (1 Sam.12:23). Prayer is just as important as witnessing. Don't neglect either for the sake of the other. Take some time right now to write out a list of at least ten people you will begin praying for daily to come to know Christ (you can do this in appendix F). Begin praying daily that God would give you opportunities to share with them and others. Also pray daily that God will make you aware of opportunities to share (Col. 4:5).

Go for it!

Ministry evangelism is probably the hardest type of evangelism. I hope these ideas make it a little easier and a whole lot more fun for you. As difficult as ministry evangelism is, it is the primary form of evangelism found in Scripture and it is the only way that we'll reach the whole world for Christ. If believers take Christ and His Great Commission seriously, they must also embrace Christ's call to go and make disciples. We can't wait for people to come to us nor share exclusively with our friends. We must actively take the Gospel to the whole earth. Remember, you don't have what it takes but the Holy Spirit in you does. Take the initiative, in the power of the Holy Spirit and then trust God to come through in the lives of those you share with!

Chapter **11**

Five
Powerful
Follow Up
Principles

"Never underestimate the power of multiplication to fulfill the Great Commission. When you totally commit yourself to a life of radical discipleship, and making disciples, you can unleash an unstoppable force...If you want to make a huge impact, implement the power of multiplication."[33] - Dave Early

Evangelistic follow up is vitally important. Most people you meet will not put their trust in Christ the first time they hear the Gospel. That means you won't see much fruit from your evangelism if you fail to follow up with those people. Following up with people is critically important. Jesus called you and me to the Great Commission, stating, "All authority in heaven and on earth has been given to me. Therefore go and make disciples of all nations, baptizing them in the name of the Father and of the Son and of the Holy Spirit, and teaching them to obey everything I have commanded you. And surely I am with you always, to the very end of the age" (Matt. 28:18-20). This command to make disciples requires a commitment to continue following up with those we share with.

In the spring of 1976, my dad and another friend were out witnessing in front of the Too Bitter Bar. They briefly witnessed to Tom Ray and invited him to a local Christian coffee house. Tom was uninterested and continued on into the bar. Later that night, as Joe Bob's bar, grill and band closed the night with the Larry Norman song, "I wish we'd all been ready," Tom couldn't help but connect the dots with what he'd heard before entering the bar. Shortly after that, God spoke clearly to him and he put hist trust in Christ in his lonely apartment. The special thing about this story is that Tom has since been a pastor for more than thirty years and he is one of the men that was most influential in my life. My dad could have easily left that conversation thinking it was a failure. it wasn't. God was working in Tom's life. Trust God to work in the lives of those you share with and do your best to continue following up with them.

After sharing the Gospel with someone, evaluate your presentation but leave the results to God. Learn how you can do better next time. There will be four possible responses after you share with someone: they might be uninterested, they may be interested, they may put their faith in Christ, or they may already be a believer. It is vitally important that you follow up with anyone who is interested, discipling young believers and continuing to witness to those who are interested but haven't yet trusted Christ!

Make the most of your window of opportunity. Satan is eager to snatch away the seed you sow (Matt. 13:19). Don't put off following up with those who are interested. They may not be interested for long. Don't be awkward or pushy, just appropriately try to schedule a time to get coffee, hang out, or meet up with anyone you have shared with that is interested. If it happens to be someone you see on a regular basis, try to make the most of those opportunities without being overbearing or weird.

Good boundaries are necessary for following up with someone you've shared with. Don't assume that if you make a mistake they won't be interested. I once set up an evangelistic follow up appointment with myself, a guy I was discipling (who I had trained to share his faith) and a non-Christian I had shared briefly with. I let the guy I was discipling do all the sharing that morning and sat there praying silently as he did one of the worst jobs sharing the Gospel that I had ever heard. I was sure we would never see the poor freshman we were reaching out to again. I was wrong. We scheduled a second appointment for the following week. Not only did the freshman student show up, he told us he had put his trust in Christ since our last appointment! Don't let your insecurities get the best of you. Make it a point to follow up with anyone that is interested, regardless of any mistakes you made.

Remember that it usually takes someone hearing the Gospel several times before they trust Christ. Your success in evangelism depends only on your obedience to share the Gospel, not the results. However, don't let that truth keep you from following up with people after sharing with them.

Everyone you share with is at a different place in relation to Christ. When you share the Gospel with someone, in a thoughtful and careful way, you'll help move them closer to Christ. Sometimes that will result in them trusting Christ but more often it brings them one step closer, with more steps to come. No matter how you look at it, every evangelistic conversation can help move someone closer and closer to Jesus. Don't believe the lie that all is lost if the person doesn't put their trust in Christ on the spot.

The Engle Scale[34] is a great way to conceptualize this issue. Every time you share the Gospel with someone, in the power of the Holy Spirit, you help that person come closer to faith in Christ, from wherever they happened to be on the Engle scale before you shared with them. Remember, hearing the Gospel is a huge deal and people usually need to think through things of such magnitude (but remember, you'll occasionally meet some who are ready to trust Christ on the spot). After sharing with someone, each successive follow up appointment should continue moving them closer and closer to trusting Christ. Again, the Engle Scale (figure 11.1) describes how you can visualize this.

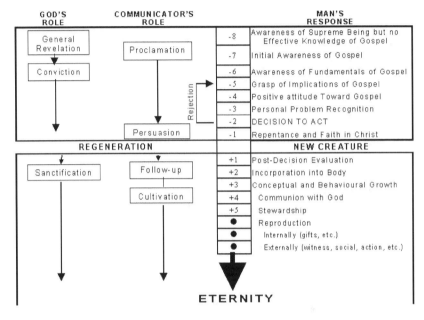

Figure 11.1

Since it usually takes several Gospel presentations before someone puts their trust in Christ, make sure to continue following up with those you witness to. The following five follow up principles will help you lead many to Christ.

First, before following up with someone you've shared with, you must evaluate how much to keep investing. Consider the following issues. Were they interested in what you shared? Did they have questions? Are they interested in meeting again? Were they open to what you said? Did they get "scared off?" Did they just want to debate? If they aren't interested that's OK, trust God to cultivate the seed you planted. Keep being friendly. Keep praying for them. Keep inviting them to things. Don't invest a tremendous amount of time following up with them if they are truly uninterested. If they are interested, keep following up with them.

Second, maintain and develop a personal connection. Make your level of commitment proportional to their level of interest. Intentionally set up an initial appointment, and remember, you only have a small window. When setting up that first appointment, you need an opening transition statement like, "what did you think of the KGP last week? Would you like to get together some time and talk more about it?" Always call them the night before to confirm and remind them of the appointment. At the end of each appointment, set up another appointment, if they're still interested. Meet them where they are at (remember 1 Cor. 9:19-23). Jesus modeled this with Zaccheus (Lk. 19) and the woman at the well (Jn. 4). Build common ground. Buy them lunch, invite them to dinner or get coffee. Do you share any hobbies? Could they join you in yours or vice versa? Could you rock climb, snowboard, play basketball or do some other activity together? What are their interests, priorities and values? Could you help them in some way? Remember, you're responsible only to be available to let God work through you in His Spirit's power, trusting the results to Him. Keep sharing your faith with all those who will really listen to you.

Third, continue clarifying the Gospel in creative ways. Don't assume they'll get it all the first time. Ask them questions. Bring up other examples, points and relevant stories conversationally. Use other modes (remember the body, relational and ministry modes). Use other tools and methods (your testimony, KGP, Soularium, the BEST FACTS, books, videos, websites, MP3s, etc). Don't just beat a dead horse, so to say, be creative about sharing the Gospel in new ways with the person you are following up with. Encourage them to begin reading the Bible (preferably have them start with the Gospel of John) and then continue asking them about it when you see them again.

Fourth, deal with objections sensitively. William Fay describes how to deal with 36 common objections to the Gospel in chapter eight of *Sharing Jesus Without Fear*.[35] Please review those so you'll be ready when those objections arise. You should probably learn some apologetics as that will equip you to defend your faith and deal with many objections that could come up (again, a great resource for that is thebestfacts.com).

Finally, fifth, remember the five Ps of following up with someone you've shared with. Trust God to bring these people to Himself over time. The five Ps are prayerful, patient, perceptive, perseverant and purposed.

Be prayerful. Put them on your top ten (or more) list and keep praying for them, even if it takes years. Also, be ready to pray for people as soon as God puts them on your heart.

Be patient. Remember God's heart, described in 2 Peter 3:9. Time is not the issue. Continue to invest in proportion to their level of interest.

Be perceptive. Be discerning and try to read where they're at and understand what their issues are. Ask God for wisdom about how to share with them.

Be perseverant. Don't give up! Keep on sharing. Have good boundaries. Respect their boundaries but don't decide for them that they aren't interested.

Be purposed. See your sphere of influence as God's plan for you. Make the most of every opportunity (Col. 4:5). No relationship is insignificant. No conversation should be either. Keep pointing to Jesus.

These five principles will lead to untold numbers of people trusting Christ. Make it your goal to follow-up with every single person you share the Gospel with and everyone that makes any contact whatsoever with your ministry.

Fulfilling the Great Commission requires that we make the most of every opportunity (Col. 4:5), not letting anyone slip through the cracks. Make sure to disciple those who come to Christ. For more on that please get my workbook *Great Commission Leadership*. Also make sure to make evangelism training part of your discipleship curriculum. It is imperative that new believers learn to share their faith right from the start. I started taking Brandon Cox out witnessing the first semester I began discipling him as a student (he and his wife Anne are now on the MPM team!). As he learned to share his faith, I began inviting him to help lead evangelism trainings with me. He caught the bug and is now committed to training others to share their faith (we even got to co-lead another evangelism training for a church last month). Make sure to disciple young believers in your sphere of influence and make sure to teach those you disciple to share their faith.

Think of a few people you've shared with in the past that you need to follow up with and come up with a follow up plan. Begin praying for them and trust God to continue working in their lives. I've seen students that have been followed up with for years end up coming to Christ. I'm sure you'll find the same to be true. Don't give up! Remember, you don't have what it takes but the Holy Spirit in you does. Take the initiative, in the power of the Holy Spirit and then trust God to come through in the lives of those you share with!

Chapter 12

The Top Ten Reasons to Share Your Faith

"Have you no wish for others to be saved? Then you're not saved yourself, be sure of that!"[36] - Charles Spurgeon

So we've come to the end of this book. I know your heart's desire is to see people come to Christ. If that weren't the case you wouldn't have made it this far. You're probably saturated with more information on this topic than you've ever had in your life. Now comes the real danger. This danger is more debilitating than any fear of evangelism ever was. It is more insidious than any attack Satan could ever level at you. It is more disastrous than the harshest consequences any government has ever used to try to silence believers. This danger is unbelief. Scripture tells us, "Do not merely listen to the Word, and so deceive yourselves. Do what it says" (James 1:22). The danger with any book like this is that you'll get a lot of great information based on a solid biblical foundation yet leave it unapplied. God's Word tells us that will lead to deception and unbelief. It always does. When I know I should share my faith, yet fail to do so, I begin to rationalize, convincing myself of the lie that people aren't interested. When I do share my faith, I get to see God come through and I become convinced of the truth that the harvest is ripe (Matt. 9:37). For this reason, I want to conclude this book with the top ten reasons you should share your faith. Here they are.

The tenth most important reason you should share your faith: you'll make new friends. As you share your faith, you'll make countless new friends with those you witness to. You'll undoubtedly meet other Christians while sharing. You'll also get to befriend those you lead to Christ. One of my best friends is a guy my room mate and I led to Christ my freshman year of college. Finally, you'll develop good friendships with non-Christians as well. There are numerous atheists, Muslims, Mormons and people of other worldviews who I have befriend through evangelism over the years. Share your faith and you'll find you have countless more friends than you ever did before.

The ninth most important reason you should share your faith: you'll have fellowship with other believers. Evangelism unites believers like nothing else. As you share your faith along with other Christian friends you'll experience life-changing fellowship. My friend Michael calls me each time he visits Durango, inviting me to go witnessing with him. His friendship, accountability and encouragement are invaluable. MPM staff lady Stephanie Brown is constantly taking the girls she disciples out witnessing. That has developed incredibly strong relationships with those girls and a couple of their friends have even come to Christ. Stephanie's passion for teaching others to share their faith, and doing it together with them, is a perfect illustration of how evangelism multiplies fellowship with other Christians. Make it a point to do evangelism in community, sharing as often as possible accompanied by other believing friends. This will lead to mutual encouragement and growth. Of course, take the initiative to share your faith whenever you can, with or without anyone else.

The eighth most important reason you should share your faith: you'll crush your fears, expand your comfort zones and grow as a person. Nothing screams "trust God" like evangelism. As you take steps of faith your faith grows stronger and stronger. That is always the case with evangelism. Evangelism is a major catalyst for personal and spiritual growth. Share your faith and you're guaranteed to grow as a person.

The seventh most important reason you should share your faith: you'll experience a life of purpose. So many Christians are literally wasting their lives and talents, spending more time trying to be entertained than living with a purpose. As you develop a habit of sharing your faith you'll escape that monotony. When you begin to see every day as an evangelistic opportunity, you'll acquire a new zest and appreciation for life.

The sixth most important reason you should share your faith: you'll experience the abundant life Jesus promised in John 10:10. So many Christians live such boring lives. Evangelism is the greatest adventure of the Christian life; partnering with God to produce eternally lasting fruit is exhilarating. Do you want to live on the front lines of the battle that you're guaranteed will be won? Then, start sharing your faith.

The fifth most important reason you should share your faith: it is the only way the world will be reached and the Great Commission accomplished. Jesus gave you and me the Great Commission two-thousand years ago (Matt. 28:18-20). It could literally be accomplished in our lifetimes through the process of spiritual multiplication (see our ministry funnel diagram, in appendix G, for more on how to do this practically and get my other book, *Great Commission Leadership*, for training on spiritual multiplication). The Great Commission begins with evangelism (you can't disciple a non-Christian!). Recently, during our Great Commission Leadership workshop (find out more about these at greatcommissionleadership.com/workshop.html), **MPM** staff member Scott Slade was out witnessing with Julie, one of the participants. They shared the Gospel with a young lady, in a park in Durango. The young lady joyfully trusted Christ. As they were speaking, two Jehovah's Witnesses came by witnessing as well. Scott was able to talk with them while Julie kept sharing with the young lady. Imagine if they hadn't been there! The harvest is ripe and the need is urgent.

The fourth most important reason you should share your faith: eternity will be changed! So many believers fail to realize that hell is real and that people you know and love are headed there now. They even try to manipulate God's Word to make it sound like evangelism will produce no real change in eternity. What a destructive, demotivating lie. Scripture is very clear that God wants all to be saved (1 Tim. 2:4), none to perish (2 Peter 3:9) and that people must have the Gospel preached to them in order for them to experience salvation (Rom. 10:13-15). Any theology that denies those truths is a lie from Satan meant to keep you from sharing your faith. Start sharing your faith and know confidently that eternity will be changed as a result of your obedience.

The third most important reason you should share your faith: you'll avoid the unbelief that has plagued so many. As you put God's Word into practice, applying it in your life, you'll see Him come through in ways most only dream of. Your unbelief will wither and your faith will grow strong. You'll be an encouragement to all those around you, helping them escape the doubt that they are mired in. Share your faith and you'll destroy the crippling sin of unbelief.

The second most important reason you should share your faith: you'll experience unparalleled intimacy with Jesus! Jesus said that those who love Him will follow His commands (John 14:15). As you share your faith you'll be loving God the way He desires to be loved and that step towards Him will be reciprocated (James 4:8). You'll experience an intimacy with God that most Christians are unaware of.

Finally, the most important reason you should share your faith: because Jesus said to. Jesus is your Lord, your Savior and your best friend. How could you possibly tell Him, "no?" How could you possibly rationalize away something so dear to His heart? Decide today to share your faith, knowing that your Lord, Savior and best friend Jesus has told you to do it. That should be reason enough (but there are countless other good reasons as well).

I am confident that this book will help you live a lifestyle of evangelism in the power of the Holy Spirit. My friend Craig Stirling has demonstrated that as long as I've known him. Whether we're snowboarding, body-boarding, running errands, or something else, he always manages to get into evangelistic conversations with virtually everyone he meets. I hope you'll allow the Holy Spirit to permeate your life and conversations in a similar way. I hope the ideas shared in this book become a part of your daily life.

I hope these ten reasons to share your faith encourage you to get out and witness today! Find a few good friends who will keep you accountable to share your faith and go witnessing together. Start an evangelism group at your church. Learn more about evangelism (again, please read my other book *Great Commission Leadership* for invaluable ministry training). Share this book with your friends. Most of them could benefit tremendously from the evangelism training you've just completed. Whatever you do, please trust God to develop you into the evangelist He made you to be.

Remember, you don't have what it takes but the Holy Spirit in you does so take the initiative and go for it. As Bill Bright said, "Success in witnessing is simply taking the initiative to share Christ in the power of the Holy Spirit and leaving the results to God. The only way we ever fail in our witness is if we fail to witness."[37]

Appendices

Appendix A - Evangelism Ideas Checklist

Check each idea off the list once you've tried it.

- ☐ Meet new people and share the Gospel with them.
- ☐ Transition any conversation to the Gospel.
- ☐ Ask a few good questions.
- ☐ Share Jesus without fear.
- ☐ Share a verse.
- ☐ Share a verse reference when it comes up.
- ☐ Use someone's name to transition to the Gospel.
- ☐ Ask about church.
- ☐ Ask "how are you?"
- ☐ Follow up with someone you have shared with.
- ☐ Ask someone about their weekend.
- ☐ Tell someone how God came through for you.
- ☐ Tell someone about the struggles your trusting God with.
- ☐ Transition health complaints to the Gospel.
- ☐ Transition conversations about the news to the Gospel.
- ☐ Transition sports conversations to the Gospel.
- ☐ Transition movie conversations to the Gospel.
- ☐ Transition music conversations to the Gospel.
- ☐ Transition near death experiences to the Gospel.
- ☐ Serve at a local mission or soup kitchen.
- ☐ Meet a specific practical or financial need.
- ☐ Buy a homeless person a meal.
- ☐ Organize a help day.
- ☐ Organize a giveaway.
- ☐ Organize a job fair.
- ☐ Raise money for a cause.
- ☐ Go on a mission trip.
- ☐ Sponsor a child.
- ☐ Reach your neighbors for Christ.
- ☐ Reach your workplace for Christ.
- ☐ Say you're sorry.
- ☐ Reach bored people for Christ.
- ☐ Invite someone to church.
- ☐ Wear a Christian t-shirt.
- ☐ Buy someone lunch.
- ☐ Tell someone Jesus loves them.
- ☐ Ask someone if you can pray for them.
- ☐ Share the Gospel in your status updates and tweets.
- ☐ Use good evangelism apps.
- ☐ Share an evangelistic website.
- ☐ Be an online missionary.
- ☐ Share the Gospel with a stranger online right now.
- ☐ Comment on an online news story.
- ☐ Share the Gospel in a Facebook ad.
- ☐ Reach people for Christ with a QR code.
- ☐ Start a blog.
- ☐ Put your testimony on Youtube.
- ☐ Post a video online.
- ☐ Write a letter to the editor.

- Leave a generous tip.
- Reach a telemarketer for Christ.
- Invite your non-Christian friends to some fun.
- Share a good book.
- Share on a bus.
- Ask an officer for a ticket.
- Buy a lottery ticket.
- Take a stand.
- Host a Q&A.
- Flash Mob Evangelism.
- Invite a few friends to go witnessing after church.
- Do some garage sale evangelism.
- Reach kids for Christ.
- Reach young adults for Christ.
- Reach senior citizens for Christ.
- Reach atheists for Christ.
- Reach homosexuals for Christ.
- Reach Mormons and Jehovah's Witnesses for Christ.
- Reach Muslims for Christ.
- Reach Jewish friends for Christ.
- Reach people from Eastern religions for Christ.
- How to share your faith during New Year's celebrations.
- How to share your faith on MLK Day.
- How to share your faith during the Superbowl.
- How to share your faith on Valentine's Day.
- How to share your faith on St. Patrick's Day.
- How to share your faith on Easter.
- How to share your faith on Mother's Day.
- How to share your faith on Memorial Day.
- How to share your faith on Father's Day.
- How to share your faith on the Fourth of July.
- How to share your faith on Labor Day.
- How to share your faith on September 11th.
- How to share your faith on Halloween.
- How to share your faith on Veteran's Day.
- How to share your faith on Thanksgiving.
- How to share your faith on Christmas.
- Use a transferable conversational tool to share the Gospel.
- Use your testimony to share the Gospel.
- Use a short Spiritual interest survey to share the Gospel.
- Use the Soularium to share the Gospel.
- Use a t-shirt to share the Gospel.
- Use the Perspective cards to share the Gospel.
- Use Jesus' own words to share the Gospel.
- Use the BEST FACTS apologetics tool to share the Gospel.
- Use tracts to share the Gospel.
- Use short movies to share the Gospel.
- Use the eCube to share the Gospel.
- Use the optical illusion cards to share the Gospel.
- Use the life as we know it tool to share the Gospel.
- Use your own tools to share the Gospel.
- Use a top ten prayer list when sharing the Gospel.

Appendix B - Evangelism Ideas Journal

As you apply these evangelism ideas, keep notes below on what happened, what you learned and what you'll do differently next time.

Evangelism Idea:

What happened:

What you learned from this activity:

What you'd do differently next time:

Evangelism Idea:

What happened:

What you learned from this activity:

What you'd do differently next time:

Evangelism Idea:

What happened:

What you learned from this activity:

What you'd do differently next time:

Evangelism Idea:

What happened:

What you learned from this activity:

What you'd do differently next time:

Evangelism Idea:

What happened:

What you learned from this activity:

What you'd do differently next time:

Evangelism Idea:

What happened:

What you learned from this activity:

What you'd do differently next time:

Evangelism Idea:

What happened:

What you learned from this activity:

What you'd do differently next time:

Evangelism Idea:

What happened:

What you learned from this activity:

What you'd do differently next time:

Evangelism Idea:

What happened:

What you learned from this activity:

What you'd do differently next time:

Evangelism Idea:

What happened:

What you learned from this activity:

What you'd do differently next time:

Evangelism Idea:

What happened:

What you learned from this activity:

What you'd do differently next time:

Evangelism Idea:

What happened:

What you learned from this activity:

What you'd do differently next time:

Evangelism Idea:

What happened:

What you learned from this activity:

What you'd do differently next time:

Evangelism Idea:

What happened:

What you learned from this activity:

What you'd do differently next time:

Evangelism Idea:

What happened:

What you learned from this activity:

What you'd do differently next time:

Appendix C - Evangelism Memory Verses

Each chapter's key verse is included below for memory

James 1:22 (NIV)

Do not merely listen to the word, and so deceive yourselves. Do what it says.

Matt. 28:18-20 (NIV)

Then Jesus came to them and said, "All authority in heaven and on earth has been given to me. Therefore go and make disciples of all nations, baptizing them in the name of the Father and of the Son and of the Holy Spirit, and teaching them to obey everything I have commanded you. And surely I am with you always, to the very end of the age."

2 Timothy 4:5 (NIV)

Do the work of an evangelist, discharge all the duties of your ministry.

Colossians 4:5 (NIV)

Be wise in the way you act toward outsiders; make the most of every opportunity.

Acts 17:26-27 (NIV)

From one man he made every nation of men, that they should inhabit the whole earth; and he determined the times set for them and the exact places where they should live. God did this so that men would seek him and perhaps reach out for him and find him...

Matthew 4:19 (NIV)

"Come, follow me," Jesus said, "and I will make you fishers of men."

Matthew 9:37 (NIV)

Then he said to his disciples, "The harvest is plentiful but the workers are few."

Psalm 96:2 (NLT)

Each day proclaim the good news that he saves.

Matthew 5:16 (NIV)

In the same way, let your light shine before men, that they may see your good deeds and praise your Father in heaven.

Romans 10:13-14 (NIV)

"Everyone who calls on the name of the Lord will be saved." How, then, can they call on the one they have not believed in? And how can they believe in the one of whom they have not heard? And how can they hear without someone preaching to them?

Romans 1:16 (NIV)

I am not ashamed of the gospel, because it is the power of God for the salvation of everyone who believes...

2 Timothy 4:2 (NIV)

Preach the Word; be prepared in season and out of season; correct, rebuke and encourage - with great patience and careful instruction.

Appendix D - Testimony Worksheet

1 Peter 3:15 tells us, "always be prepared to give an answer to everyone who asks you to give the reason for the hope that you have." Your personal testimony, the story of what God has done in your life, is one of the best ways you can do this. Although people can try to argue about the veracity of Christianity's claims, no one can argue with what Christ has done in your life. It has been said that "a man with a testimony is never at the mercy of a man with an argument." People are often very interested in what the God of the universe is doing on a personal level and they want to know what He is doing in your life.

A testimony is most effective when it is concise, to the point and organized (see Paul's personal testimony in Acts 26 for an example).

How to organize and write your personal testimony.

Ask the Lord to guide you as you write (James 1:5).

Prepare it in such a way that you can give it to groups or individuals. Keep it concise and emphasize a personal commitment to Christ.

Consider your typical audience (those you will most often be communicating with) and write it in a way that will relate to them.

Try to keep it within a three minute time limit (see Paul's example again in Acts 26, it will take about three minutes to read).

Be realistic and honest about what you include.

Keep it focused: avoid a religious approach - do not spend much time speaking about your church activities. Avoid inappropriate details about your past. Avoid mundane details about how you grew up. Stick to a theme.

Avoid the following terminology:

Do not make statements that reflect negatively on churches, other organizations or people.

Avoid mentioning denominations.

Explain vague terms such as joyful, peaceful, happy and changed when you use them.

Explain Biblical words such as saved, born again, converted and sin when you use them (be careful not to speak "Christianese").

Write out your testimony with these key components:

Begin with an attention getting sentence or short story.

Use a three point outline containing the following (your personal examples will go a long way towards establishing your credibility with your audience so be real and honest but also be appropriate):

1. What was your life like before Christ?

   a. What were your attitudes, needs and problems?

   b. What did your life revolve around? What was most important to you?

   c. What did you look to for security, peace of mind and happiness and in what ways did those leave you unsatisfied?

2. What led you to put your trust in Christ?

   a. Be very honest about how you came to that decision.

    b. Do your best to summarize the gospel at this point and how you responded to the gospel.

3. What happened after you received Christ?

    a. Contrast who you were before with who you are now and focus on the change God has produced and is continuing to produce in your life.

Only use phrases, questions and examples that are natural and won't make your audience tense or uncomfortable.

Be positive from start to finish.

Keep the emphasis and focus on Christ throughout your testimony.

Be specific. Give enough details to arouse curiosity (but remember to be appropriate and to not overemphasize your sin - keep the emphasis on Christ).

Be natural. Do your best to help people understand and know you.

Be accurate and honest.

Include relevant, thought provoking experiences.

Use one or two Scripture references but only when they relate directly to your experience and fit naturally in your testimony.

Don't end your testimony with a verse but rather keep Scripture in the body of your testimony.

End with a well thought through closing.

Edit your testimony and rewrite it as much as needed to get it just right. Then memorize it so you will "always being ready to make a defense to everyone who asks you to give an account for the hope

101 Easy, Effective and Exciting Evangelism Ideas

that is in you." Then use it often!

Write out your testimony on the next page and then edit and memorize. Time yourself to see if you're close to the three minute target. Look for opportunities to use your testimony in evangelistic conversations. Also ask the person discipling you to schedule a time for you to share it publicly.

Write out your personal testimony!

Write an attention getting sentence or paragraph.

What was your life like before you received Christ?

What led you to put your trust in Christ, why did you give Him complete control of your life and how did you make the decision (briefly summarize the main points of the gospel here)?

What happened after you received Christ, what changes have you seen in your life?

Write a good closing.

Now, share your testimony boldly (have a friend evaluate you first to see how to improve, do this on the next page)!

Testimony Evaluation (have someone evaluate you):

Did the testimony begin with an attention getting introduction? How could this improve?

Did the person clearly and appropriately describe their life before Christ? How could this improve?

Did the person explain how they came to the point of putting their trust in Christ? How could this improve?

Was the Gospel clearly described (God's love, man's sin, Jesus' payment, personal need, point of decision)? How could this improve?

Did the person clearly describe how Christ has changed their life and how their life today contrasts with their life before Christ?

Did the testimony end on time? How long was it supposed to go and how long did it go (if it was a typical three minute testimony, did they do it in three minutes)?

How was their presentation (smile, voice projection, tone, pace, body language, eye contact, etc.) and what could improve?

Did the speaker speak passionately and boldly and how could they improve?

Were there any distracting mannerisms or filler words (uh, um, OK, right, like, etc.) that should be avoided next time? List them (mannerisms and/or filler words):

How can this person improve as a speaker?

What was your favorite part about this testimony?

How would you like to encourage this person about their testimony?

Appendix E - More Great Evangelism Ideas

Sites:

1. spreadtruth.com/resources
2. e3resources.org
3. evangelismexplosion.org/resources
4. crupressgreen.com
5. store.livingwaters.com
6. missionalwomen.com
7. eternityimpact.com
8. greatcommissionleadership.com
9. evangelismcoach.org
10. internetevangelismday.com

Books:

1. *Great Commission Leadership* by Nate Herbst
2. *Hell's Best Kept Secret* by Ray Comfort
3. *Share Jesus Without Fear* by William Fay and Linda Evans Shepherd
4. *The 250; Creative Ideas for Evangelism* by Cru Press
5. *Tactics: A Game Plan for Discussing Your Christian Convictions* by Gregory Koukl
6. *The Finishers* by Roger Hershey and Jason Weimer
7. One Thing You Can't do in Heaven by Mark Cahill
8. *Reach; How to Use Your Social Media Influence for the Glory of God* by Laura Krokos and Angi Pratt
9. *Evangelism Is - How to Share Jesus with Passion and Confidence* by Dave Earley and David Wheeler
10. *Family to Family, Leaving a Lasting Legacy* by Dr. Jerry Pipes and Victor Lee

Do your own search! There are a ton of great resources out there.

Appendix F - Top 10 List

List the top ten non-Christians you're trusting Christ will bring to Himself. Under each one's name, include notes of your previous evangelistic conversations and how you intend to continue following up with them.

1. _____

2. _____

3. _____

4. _____

5. _____

6. _____

7. _____

8. _____

9. _____

10._____

Appendix G - The Funnel Diagram

This diagram explains a spiritual multiplication strategy that can be implemented anywhere. You can remember this with the IMPACT acronym (Intercession, Meet new people, Preach the Gospel, Active discipleship, Context of love, Tools).

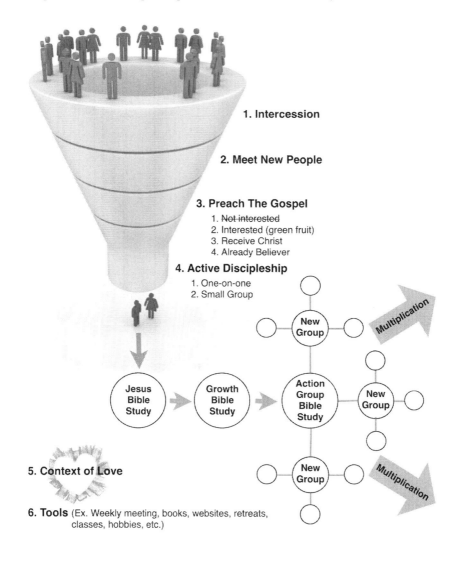

1. Intercession

2. Meet New People

3. Preach The Gospel
   1. Not interested
   2. Interested (green fruit)
   3. Receive Christ
   4. Already Believer

4. Active Discipleship
   1. One-on-one
   2. Small Group

Jesus Bible Study

Growth Bible Study

Action Group Bible Study

New Group

Multiplication

5. Context of Love

6. Tools (Ex. Weekly meeting, books, websites, retreats, classes, hobbies, etc.)

Appendix H - Great Commission Leadership

Get Nate's other book, *Great Commission Leadership* on Amazon. It is a workbook designed to equip you to do the Great Commission. You could also come to one of our GCL workshops (find out more at http://greatcommissionleadership.com/workshop.html).

Endnotes

[1] Bill Bright, "*Sharing with Confidence*," http://www.cru.org/training-and-growth/sharing-with-confidence.htm (accessed January 3, 2013)

[2] The Traveling Team, "*Growth of the Church*," http://www.thetravelingteam.org/node/192 (Accessed January 31, 2013).

[3] Islam Watch, "*Islam Under Scrutiny by Ex-Muslims*," http://www.islam-watch.org/LeavingIslam/Muslims2Christianity.htm (Accessed Jan 31, 2013).

[4] The Williams Brothers, "*I'm Just a Nobody Lyrics*," http://www.lyricsondemand.com/w/williamsbrotherslyrics/imjustanobodylyrics.html (accessed June 18, 2014)

[5] Keith Davy, "*Evangelism Model - Modes Component*," http://www.aggiecru.com/wp-content/uploads/2010/06/NotesforTeachingEvangelismModel.pdf (accessed January 17, 2013)

[6] W. Y. Fullerton, "*Charles Haddon Spurgeon: A Biography*," http://www.spurgeon.org/misc/bio11.htm (accessed July 20, 2014)

[7] Bill Bright, "*Sharing with Confidence*," http://www.cru.org/training-and-growth/sharing-with-confidence.htm (accessed January 3, 2013)

[8] Penn Jillette, "*Penn Jillette gets a gift of a Bible*," http://www.youtube.com/watch?v=ZhG-tkQ_Q2w (accessed January 13, 2013)

[9] Gregory Koukl, *Tactics: A Game Plan for Discussing Your Christian Convictions* (Grand Rapids, MI: Zondervan, 2009), 31.

[10] Dave Earley and David Wheeler, *Evangelism Is - How to Share Jesus with Passion and Confidence* (Nashville, TN: B and H Publishing Group, 2010), 3.

[11] Keith Davy, *Passages: A Devotional Journey* (Orlando, FL: CruPress, 2008), 19.

[12] William Fay and Linda Evans Shepherd, *Share Jesus Without Fear* (Nashville, TN: Broadman and Holman Publishers, 1999).

[13] Dave Earley and David Wheeler, *Evangelism Is - How to Share Jesus with Passion and Confidence* (Nashville, TN: B and H Publishing Group, 2010).

[14] C.H. Spurgeon, *An All Around Ministry: Addresses to Ministers and Students* (BookAndSuchNW, 2009), Ch. 4, Kindle.

[15] Mark Batterson, *All In: You Are One Decision Away From a Totally Different Life* (Grand Rapids, MI: Zondervan, 2013), 13.

[16] Thom S. Rainer, *The Unchurched Next Door: Understanding Faith Stages as Keys to Sharing Your Faith* (Grand Rapids, MI: Zondervan, 2003), 24.

[17] David Platt, *Radical: Taking Back Your Faith from the American Dream* (Colorado Springs, CO: Multnomah, 2010), 83.

[18] Laura Krokos and Angi Pratt, Reach; *How to Use Your Social Media Influence for the Glory of God* (Reachbook.com, 2012).

[19] The Traveling Team, "*Growth of the Church,*" http://www.thetravelingteam.org/node/192 (Accessed January 31, 2013).

[20] Islam Watch, "*Islam Under Scrutiny by Ex-Muslims,*" http://www.islam-watch.org/LeavingIslam/Muslims2Christianity.htm (Accessed Jan 31, 2013).

[21] Mark Cahill, *One Thing You Can't do in Heaven* (Biblical Rockwall, TX: Discipleship Publishers, 2002), 11.

[22] Lee Strobel, *The Case for Christ* (Grand Rapids, MI: Zondervan Publishing House,1998).

[23] Norm Geisler and Frank Turek, *I Don't Have Enough Faith to be an Atheist* (Wheaton, IL: Crossway Books, 2004).

[24] Mark Cahill, *One Thing You Can't do in Heaven* (Biblical Rockwall, TX: Discipleship Publishers, 2002), 73.

[25] Norm Geisler and Frank Turek, *I Don't Have Enough Faith to be an Atheist* (Wheaton, IL: Crossway Books, 2004).

[26] Nabeel A. Querishi, *Seeking Alah, Finding Jesus* (Grand Rapids, MI: Zondervan, 2014).

27 Islam Watch, "*Islam Under Scrutiny by Ex-Muslims*," http://www.islam-watch.org/LeavingIslam/Muslims2Christianity.htm (Accessed Jan 31, 2013).

28 Ed Hindson and Ergun Caner, *The Popular Encyclopedia of Apologetics: Surveying the Evidence for the Truth of Christianity* (Eugene, OR: Harvest House Publishers, 2008).

29 Ravi Zacharias, *The Lotus and the Cross* (Colorado Springs, CO: Multnomah Books, 2001).

30 Roger Hershey and Jason Weimer, The Finishers, (Orlando, FL: CruPress, 2011), 197.

31 Lee Strobel, *The Case for Easter: A Journalist Investigates the Evidence for the Resurrection* (Grand Rapids, MI: Zondervan, 2014).

32 Gregory Koukl, *Tactics: A Game Plan for Discussing Your Christian Convictions* (Grand Rapids, MI: Zondervan, 2009), 31.

33 Dave Earley and Rod Dempsey, *Disciple Making Is . . .: How to Live the Great Commission with Passion and Confidence* (Nashville, TN: B&H Publishing Group, 2013), 118.

34 James Engle, *What's Gone Wrong With the Harvest* (Grand Rapids, MI: Zondervan, 1975).

35 William Fay and Linda Evans Shepherd, *Share Jesus Without Fear* (Nashville, TN: Broadman and Holman Publishers, 1999), 81-112.

36 Charles H. Spurgeon, "Quotable Quotes," http://www.goodreads.com/quotes/154682-have-you-no-wish-for-others-to-be-saved-then (accessed January 24, 2013)

37 Bill Bright, "*Sharing with Confidence*," http://www.cru.org/training-and-growth/sharing-with-confidence.htm (accessed January 3, 2013)

Keep up the fight!

Made in the USA
San Bernardino, CA
09 December 2014

17377016R00105